THE ULTIMATE
CHIROPRACTIC PRACTICE

How You Can Double Your Income in 60 Days or Less Without Feeling Overwhelmed

Written by
Dr. Dennis Short, D.C.
For
The Ultimate Chiropractic L.L.C.

outskirtspress
DENVER, COLORADO

Outskirts Press, Inc.
http://www.outskirtspress.com

ISBN: 978-1-4327-9533-7

Library of Congress Control Number: 2012911712

Outskirts Press and the "OP" logo are trademarks belonging to Outskirts Press, Inc.

PRINTED IN THE UNITED STATES OF AMERICA

A Word from Douglas R. Andrew

The Ultimate Chiropractic Practice is an "absolute must-read" book for Chiropractors who want to dramatically transform their practice and take it to an entirely new level of success.

Chiropractors will experience a meaningful transformation in their practice through Dennis Short's powerful process as he reveals the secrets that led to his success.

Dr. Dennis Short will help you gain greater clarity, balance, focus and confidence in your life.

Through Dennis Short's leadership and masterful communication, he provides new direction, confidence and capability to the Chiropractic professional's pursuit for excellence.

Get ready to gain tremendous insights that will transform your life, your practice, your patient's lives and your true wealth for generations.

Douglas R. Andrew
New York Times and Wall Street Journal
Best-selling author of the Missed Fortune book series

Table of Contents

PART I

Introduction

School rarely prepares us completely for real life. The sting of that statement hits doctors harder than most. We dedicate our high school and undergraduate education in the quest for high grades, just so we can get accepted into a graduate program. Our close friends who choose different paths are enjoying their youth partying, making money, getting married and later, raising a family. One can't help question our sanity as to why we committed our life to service. But, we press on.

We tell ourselves, "It will be all worth it in the end. When I graduate and get into private practice, things will be better. Life will be better!" We study hard in graduate school to get good grades and prepare for the government exams. Our success hinges on getting satisfactory standing on these board exams. So, we press on – and the hopeful voice inside echoes more.

"It will be all worth it when we get out into private practice."

At first, we believed this statement with every fiber of our being. But now, as the end of school draws near, we start to question ourselves again. We know higher-class mates who are living the life after school, and they struggle financially and are being abused by more senior doctors.

Your friends are not really seeing patients; they are only doing things the senior doctors don't want to do. But, we press on.

"It will be all worth it when we get out into private practice."

Whether the statement is a lie or the truth doesn't matter. We have to keep saying it to convince our minds to stick with it. If we don't stick with it, how will we ever pay off these student loans? You may be thinking, "If I only knew then what I know now, I would have never kept going to school."

Your high school friends have 10 years in a good job by now and have 5-year-old children. You long for their life so much you can almost taste it.

People are starting to ask you what you are going to do after graduation, but you don't really know. Some tell you that you should move to a town that has the best money-making opportunity, while others tell you not to sell your soul for money, but to go to the area you would most like to live. This confusion only fuels your doubt even more. So you ask, "Why didn't I work in the factory after high school?"

The day finally comes. You have finished all of your school exams. You have passed all your government exams. You can practice anywhere you want. But, where? Your elation overpowers your confusion. You are ready to walk that stage and receive that diploma. Your school says you are ready, the government says you are ready, your state licensing board says you are ready, society at large says you are ready, but you think, "There is no way I'm ready."

When the world thinks you are something, but deep down inside, you think otherwise, you feel like a fraud. You have done an excellent job, but only at pulling the wool over the world's eyes. They may call you doctor, but you feel like nobody.

But, we press on.

Most students feel this way after graduation. And this often results in the frightened puppy syndrome. They go looking for work and more seasoned doctors can smell the fear and doubt from miles away. You still grapple with the decision to set up your own practice instead of working for someone else, but you are just not confident in your abilities. So you think, "Maybe I should just get a year or two of experience by working for Dr. X." The money sucks, but at least you can defer your student loans and get the experience you need.

You end up taking a job in Middle America for pennies, and all you are doing is mall screening. Your boss tells you that it is just temporary so you get the chance to see the marketing side of the practice. When you get a couple of months under your belt, he will train you to see patients. It is not glamorous work but necessary.

So, you press on.

Four months go by, and you see no hope of ever getting out of this mall. You build up the courage to ask your boss when you will get the chance to see patients, and they tell you after the Christmas rush. Two months later, when the boss senses you are about to quit, he starts to train you to see patients. Day in and day out, you observe him treat patients while you do exams, X-rays, and take notes.

When he senses that you have either learned enough or are so horribly discouraged, he informs you that you are ready. Come Monday morning, you will be seeing your own patients. You SHOULD also get a pay raise because now you will be getting 30% of the collections from every patient you see. All weekend, you are so excited that you call all of your family, go back and study your textbooks, or go partying because you just can't sleep. Life is finally going to kick into gear and man, have you paid your dues.

Monday morning comes and you are ready to hit the road running. You ask the office secretary how many patients are scheduled with you and she says, "NONE." How is that possible? You go to your boss to see where the mistake happened.

He informs you that you have to get your own patients, because there is no way his patients will see a doctor with so little experience. Who wants bronze when you can have gold?

You don't know what to do so you decide to stick it out, and you do manage to drum up a few patients over the next month. You have been treating them, they are getting well and your confidence is growing daily. Then, payday arrives and you get a check for $457.42. What the #@%#$? Apparently, you lost your low-base wage when you started seeing patients. The $457.42 was your 30% of your collections for the whole month.

All weekend, your mind starts to wonder. "I know all I need to know," you think. "I can start my own office and do better than that."

You beg, borrow, or steal what you have to and start the process of opening your own office. You decide to move closer to your family because they can at least be your first patients.

It takes six months to open your office. It cost $136,000 but at least it is new, modern, and state of the art. You open your office and the first patients are your mom, dad, sister, brother and anyone else you can convince to come in.

Some of these offices succeed. But, here's a cold, hard look at sobering reality: According to statistics, 95% will fail in three years. That's the cold, hard truth.

And only three of every 10 chiropractors who graduate are still in practice three years later. Talk about a profession that is in severe need for an adjustment.

I positively hate to write the above statistics. It makes me feel like a failure just writing the words. I know many doctors who fall into this or similar scenarios. I am sickened by how much failure there is in our wonderful profession. We have one of the greatest gifts to give, yet we can't seem to package it or sell it, or overcome the opposition that still seems to exist in other channels of medicine. Even if we do seem to have the skill to sell it, we often get burned out or can't maintain our hectic life.

Why? I have been asking myself that question for years. And after owning a very successful office and opening five other successful satellite offices, I think I can help my readers better understand why some doctors are successful in the chiropractic profession as compared to others who are struggling.

This book hopefully will enlighten you about the physical and metaphysical principles of chiropractic success. The principles that I cover are not only for chiropractors, but for anyone wishing to expand any business successfully. The principles that I talk about have aided veterinarians, massage therapists, and acupuncturists. For that reason, I have no doubt these principles can assist anyone to grow a business into their ideal practice.

Keep in mind that I understand hard reality. I was born into a family that had no extra money. I was not born with a silver spoon in my mouth, nor did any person who was successful inspire me. I was not divinely blessed, at least not as far as I know, and I do not think that I am better than anyone else. My family and I have become successful, and we have done it all by ourselves, and with the great systems already in place in America. I do not say these words to stroke my ego. I say them because I am no one special.

And if I can go from rags to riches, then anyone can.

Being born in a society that assists its poor citizens to become educated is a blessing. Without a student loan, there is no way I would be where I am today. Too often, we forget about this wonderful country we live in and I hope that I remind you about how lucky we really are.

Running a busy and profitable chiropractic office is not easy. An office comprises many facets, and, being the leader of the business, you have to wear many hats and have big shoes to fill. My job is to give you the tools and strategies to make your life less complex and give you more certainty. Not only would I like to give you some of the knowledge necessary to operate a profitable office, I would also like to assist you in growing long-term wealth.

It has been said, "Ignorance is bliss." Whoever authored that statement deserves to be punished. Ignorance is not bliss. In fact, ignorance is pain and poverty. Let me teach you how to stop the pain and increase your wealth.

1

The Pyramid of Chiropractic Success

In school, we all had an idea about what it took to become successful in the chiropractic business. We all thought that technique was king. We argued with our peers for hours about what was the best way to perform the chiropractic adjustment. We all thought we had the truth, and we figured anyone who thought differently was only deluding himself or herself. We thought that practicing doctors who performed our technique were successful while others using inferior techniques were destined to struggle in business. When a doctor who practiced a different technique was successful, we figured it was only because the doctor was such a good sales person that he or she could convince poor patients to pay for his or her version of hocus-pocus.

The Bible states in 1 Corinthians 13:11 , "When I was a child, I talked like a child, I thought like a child, I reasoned like a child. When I became a man, I put childish ways behind me." The thought that one person has the truth while all others don't is a childish thought pattern. I have been to many chiropractic offices that are successful. They are enhancing millions of people's lives and they are all practiced differently. Your technique means next to nothing. I know these words shock many doctors, but it is true. If one technique were better than another, then failure would be based on technique. I have seen all types of practitioners using all types of techniques go out of business. I say again, "your technique means nothing."

Once I discovered this truth, I wanted to determine what the actual factors were that determined success. Over the years, I have studied many doctors and have set up many of my own offices. And I believe that I am closer now than ever before to determining the true factors leading to chiropractic and business success.

I placed these factors in a pyramid to illustrate the relative value of each. Principles closer to the bottom are more foundational and important, creating a great platform for growth.

I have asked many doctors to identify keys to their success. And while they may have given me different words to describe that success, their basic truth remained related to my pyramid. On occasion, I have observed doctors who have operated contrary to these principles, and yet appeared to have a successful office. When I see these enigmas, I make a point to dig deeper to possibly learn from them. On closer observation, I have noticed deficits in their business that will surely result in their demise. I will explain some of these examples throughout the body of this and following chapters.

Figure 1. Illustrates **The Pyramid of Chiropractic Success**, which has 8 categories. There are many subcategories to each level and I will tackle them individually with a detailed look at the importance of each.

Figure I.
The Pyramid of Chiropractic Success

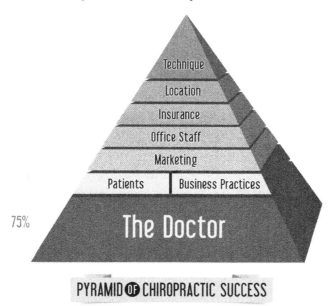

Because I believe that the majority of problems in a non-successful office lie with the doctor, I will spend the bulk of this book writing about the roles a doctor must master in order to expand an office. But first, I will give a brief outline of **The Pyramid of Chiropractic Success**.

The doctor consumes 75% of this diagram because, when an office is a monumental success, you can invariably find a doctor who is in complete control. Just as a house cannot stand without a strong foundation, the chiropractic office cannot long survive without a strong doctor/leader. They are the leader and the figurehead of the organization. They are the one who possesses the infectious personality, yet still manages to demand respect. The community trust is placed firmly on the leader's shoulders, and he or she is the one that is generally called by other community leaders when they want to get something done.

Inside the office, they are the one the staff looks to for guidance. They are the troubleshooter and the one who always stays cool during confrontation. He or she is the one who has created an office culture, an atmosphere of structured growth and a clear chain of command.

The patients see them as an ocean of information and the one who supplies direction in their health plan. They are the pictures of integrity. They live, breathe and eat what they preach. They are committed to the cause and no one questions his/her position of authority.

I have aided many doctors in growing their business, and I can tell you that there is no purpose in trying to make a doctor successful if the doctor does not see that they are the keystone to success or possibly the weak link resulting in failure. The doctor who does not see this truth is bound to struggle forever.

The remaining 25% of this pyramid is constructed of a more traditional business concept. These concepts are generally foreign to chiropractic doctors. Because of the lack of business education, these business fundamentals may be the missing link to your chiropractic success.

The next category is called, "Patients & Business Practices." These two categories are not really related, but I decided to place them together for a very good reason. I believe that it is more important to have great business practices rather than lots of patients. Patient volume will ebb and flow resulting in economic turmoil, but with good, sound business practices, you will be more equipped to harbor the storm. However, I must be pragmatic. I have known many successful doctors who have had poor business practice, but they compensate by having a large patient base.

Recently, I aided a chiropractor who wanted to expand his office and create a franchise. He already had a booming office and was obviously successful. However, during our in-depth conversations, I started to talk about specific business practices, and I could see his eyes glaze over in confusion. So I had to ask. "You don't do these statistics in your office, do you?" He admitted his guilt, and I started lecturing him on the importance of running an efficient office.

I see his office as a big bucket of water. His current success was mainly due to a large influx of new patients (water), and even though he had a big leak in the bottom of his bucket, he managed to grow and his bucket runs over from the influx of new patients. I warned him that all businesses go through rough patches and he needed to clean up his actions or, if the new patient volume ever decreased, he would be in danger. He stated that he was not interested in all that, but just wanted to expand. So I helped him with his goal.

A year later, he contacted me again, wanting to learn more because his office had taken a nosedive with the decrease in the economy. Trying to repair a sinking ship is difficult. It would have been better if he took my advice a year prior. He would have been able to weather the storm with less rough seas. I'm happy to say that we did help him and he did not go out of business. But we estimate that he may have lost $500,000.

This story is told to show you that it is possible to have poor business skills and still succeed in practice. But it is risky. To endure the hard times, which always come, one must have a strong business mind. Sure, the doctor in the story was successful, even though he had no business sense, when he had a massive influx of clients. And that is a testament to how great our profession and this country really are. But, we are going through some tough times and we have to become stronger if we are to survive this new economy.

The best combination is to have great business practices as well as a large new patient base. That is the combination of the extremely affluent, and it can be your combination as well.

Next in **The Pyramid Of Chiropractic Success** is marketing. There is not a day that goes by that I don't get junk mail in my email account that tells me, "They have the key to marketing." This is my least favorite topic. However, I do think it is important to market yourself. There are many ways to do effective marketing. External marketing deals with marketing outside of your office via radio, advertisements, billboards or public speaking. Internal marketing deals with getting your patients to refer their family and friends.

I prefer to do internal marketing, because it is much cheaper, more predictable and you generally get a higher quality of patient for your efforts. There are many ways to accomplish internal marketing. We will address those in later chapters.

Marketing is one area that many chiropractors struggle with. We need new patients in order to survive, but we do not wish to come across to the general public as shady or unscrupulous. Balancing this fine line can be tricky, extremely expensive, unproductive, and possibly illegal.

Number 4 on the pyramid is office staff. Your staff can either make you or break you. They are the first and last encounter for your patients. I have seen many chiropractors put up with horrible staff because they never had the guts to let them go. Being a business owner is not for the weak at heart. Besides, if they are not good at their job in your office, you are doing them a favor by firing them. By pushing them out of the nest, maybe they can find a career that better suits their temperament.

My motto is, "quick to hire and quick to fire." The longer you let your staff permeate a bad attitude through your office, the more difficult it will be to clean up their mess when you eventually do let them go.

On a different note, I am rarely forced to tell a doctor that they have to fire a staff person. Poor staff is generally a factor of poor education and poor leadership by the doctor, and we will talk more about this in future chapters. Most things can be corrected, but remember, there is no cure for a bad personality or stupidity.

It is common to see a husband and wife combination in our profession. The man goes to chiropractic school to become a doctor and the wife runs the front office. This combination rarely works. It will eventually either cause problems at work or in the home. There must be a clear chain of command in a business, and no wife likes to be bossed around by her husband. I will not take an office under my wing that has this arrangement. The outcomes are too unpredictable and will only tarnish my reputation as a business expansion expert.

Next on the **Pyramid of Chiropractic Success** is insurance. I have known many doctors who are successful with cash practices. Insurance is by no means a must in order to have the practice of your dreams. To be honest, the practice of my dreams would be without documentation and delayed payment, which means a cash practice is the way to go.

However, I do accept insurance in my office for two main reasons. First those with insurance pay better than cash patients, so I can make more money with less effort, and second, I was not called to this profession to satisfy my needs; I was called to serve the patient and the patient is best served by accepting their insurance.

In the chapter on insurance, I will tell you how to properly diagnose, code, document and bill insurance to get maximum returns without worrying about the risk of audits.

I will not accept a coaching position for an office that does not accept insurance. It's not that I don't agree with the concept in principle; it is simply that it tells me something about the doctor. It is my contention that any doctor who does not accept insurance is in practice for themselves, not for the patient. We are not here to make the patient's life harder. Not accepting their insurance makes it difficult for the average, penny-pinching American. Sure, it is more work, but it generally pays more and I do not define myself as someone who takes the lazy road.

The 6th position on the **Pyramid of Chiropractic Success** is location. I have owned offices in poor locations and I have owned offices that had the best location in town. From all of my experience, I have learned that great locations can get the doctor lots of new patients but it cannot make up for a poor quality doctor.

A large influx of new patients is a great thing when you are new in practice, and to an extent, it can compensate for costly, external marketing. Once you are in town for more than a year, your location doesn't matter much. If you have done your work right, everyone in town knows where you are and the location has little to do with continued growth. Doctors who are used to having a constant flow of new patients into their office while they are new in practice get spoiled. They mismanage patients and don't focus on internal marketing. They expect that the new patients will keep coming until one day they stop. This is extremely frustrating and new doctors have no idea how to make a comeback.

Last and certainly least is technique. I know this will ruffle some of your feathers. When I first learned it, mine were definitely ruffled, too, but let me explain. I am by no means advocating that you can do anything to a patient and still grow an office. You have to be effective, you have to produce results. So, in that way, your technique is the most important tool you have. But, many different practitioners are successful with a rainbow of different techniques. The type of technique is not as important as the careful execution of the technique and skill of the doctor, as well as his or her ability to sell his unique system.

There are, however, some techniques that are harder to

sell than others. The more you sway away from the mainstream of what the general population considers chiropractic, the more difficult it is to sell. Chiropractic practice is a numbers game. If you are practicing in farm country, and you want to practice an upper cervical, specific technique, you may have a following of 10 people. There will always be people that see life your way, but will there be enough people to grow a practice? You are always better using well-established chiropractic techniques for the general public. And if you have a passion for another technique, practice it on a few patients who are more along your wavelength.

The point of the story is that you must be a master of your technique, no matter which one it is. If your technique is off the beaten path of chiropractic and you are set on using solely that and none else in your office, make sure that you are in an area that is open to it or has a great enough population that even a small percentage of the people still equals thousands of patients.

There is a quick synopsis of **The Pyramid of Chiropractic Success**. As I said earlier, there are many great chiropractors who have been successful without knowing this pyramid. But if you ask them to give you a detailed guide to their success, you will see very similar elements.

As a comparison, I will create a pyramid that is consistent with most of the thought patterns you probably held dear once you graduated from chiropractic college. I am not pompous enough to speak for every new chiropractor, but I once had this same mentality, and not until I had substantial experience in practice did I begin to see the error of my ways.

Figure 2.
The Student's Pyramid of Chiropractic Success

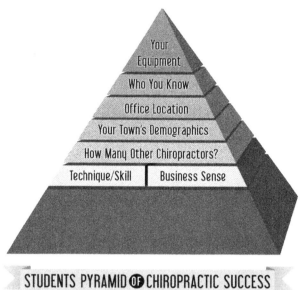

School gave us the thought pattern that we were God's gift to the health care system's problems. We thought we would be accepted by the general public with open arms. Our offices would be full instantly with eager patients just waiting to be touched by us and our training. Man, were we wrong.

Because of the above mentality, it is not hard to discovery why the average new chiropractor believes that the keys to success are technical. We worry: "Is my technique better than other chiropractors? Will there be other chiropractors in my town? What quality chiropractic adjusting table will I buy? Can I find a great location? And how can I get to know the key people in town?"

I don't want to spend too much time on this flawed pyramid. It was created simply to illustrate the mentality shift that must occur if one is to be successful in the chiropractic profession.

In the remainder of the body of this book, you will get a closer look at each of the elements in the real version of **The Pyramid of Chiropractic Success,** as well as ideas that I use when I help coach doctors to begin living successfully.

2
The Doctor

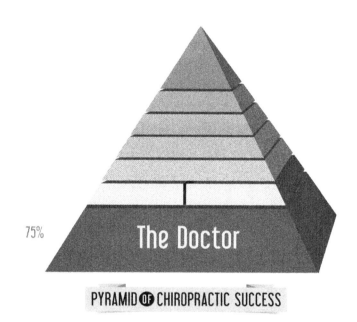

75%

The Doctor

PYRAMID OF CHIROPRACTIC SUCCESS

"It is not the strongest of the species that survive, nor the most intelligent, but the one that proves itself most responsive to change."

—Charles Darwin

The true definition of the label "doctor" is teacher. This is a person whom people come to for knowledge and guidance. This role should not be taken lightly. Not only do you need to be a fountain of knowledge, but you also have to be able to motivate people to action. You must have confidence and an authoritative presence that instills hope for the people who follow you.

Not only is the doctor in the office the leader for the patients, they also have to be the leader for the staff. It takes a special personality to be able to take on these many roles. In this section, I will break down what I think are the key elements of a leader/doctor. To do this properly, I would have to first learn who you are. That, of course, is impossible to do in a book, but priority number one in my coaching practice. I have learned over the years that in order for a chiropractor to be successful, he or she must have great internal dialogue. Great internal dialogue allows them to have great external dialogue with the people they are meant to lead.

To help a doctor, I have to get inside their head. I have to know what makes him or her tick. I cannot simply deal with external factors. That is, of course, if one hopes to make a lasting change. Because a doctor is usually the most limiting factor in an office, I have to deal with their limitations, if I am to propel them towards success.

The first rule of business is that your business is not about you. It is not even about your product or service. It is about your customers. The people to whom you sell your services are the controlling factor of whether your business is successful or not. People have made successful businesses out of hauling garbage. As long as they do it properly and offer a good service, they will be successful.

Keep in mind that if your office business is slow, it is because people don't appreciate what you do, or that they are not aware of what you do. If they are not aware of what you do, than marketing is the answer to your problems. If they come to your office but don't stay, then you are going unappreciated. If you are unappreciated, than you have not done a good job at educating people as to what you can do and the importance of your services.

When I state that "your business is not about you," what I mean is that doctors, first of all, love to talk about themselves to their patients. Yet, actually, the patient is in your office to talk about themselves. Secondly, I often hear new doctors talk about having Fridays off and not working on the weekends or not working late. These phrases tell me that the doctor does not truly get that the business is not about making them comfortable and happy. It is about making your patients comfortable and happy. This mentality shift makes all the difference and can propel the chiropractic business rapidly forward.

The majority of what I will discuss under the heading, The Doctor, could also be described as the doctor's attitude. We have all been told that the difference between success and failure is attitude. A doctor must have the attitude of charity, success, service and a strong sense of self-worth in order to be successful. However, the term attitude is far too vague. There is no way that I could coach a doctor toward success by simply telling him or her to change their attitude. That is why I have subcategorized the doctor's personality into many different topics. Then, by tackling each aspect of the doctor's attitude, we can better modify a failure attitude to that of a winner.

Everyone's personality is composed of many different facets. How we respond when we are happy is hardly the way we respond when we are feeling pushed. There are times that we feel we can take on the world, and yet other moments when we feel like not getting out of bed. This is part of the human existence. We are not meant to feel the same way all of the time.

The specific collection of these feelings and the actions that follow make up your personality. There are definitely some commonalities with your actions and other people's, yet your complete collection is uniquely yours, and it is more unique than your fingerprints.

In the quest to become successful in your chiropractic office, you have to realize that there are common systems and habits to becoming successful, just as there are common systems and habits to business failure. Our goal throughout this book is to discover the success principles that are common to successful offices and repeat them. On the other hand, we have to discover our weakness and bad habits and stop repeating them.

This self-discovery and remodeling is necessary when you are trying to flourish in any endeavor, whether it is business, school, a relationship, religion or anything else. This is the process of growth, and there is no place better to grow than in your business. Charlie "Tremendous" Jones once said "you can't be better with your family unless you are better with your business, and you can't be better with your business until you are better with your family. They complement each other." I believe that statement with all of my heart. I have seen money struggles and the feeling of failure destroy more marriages than success ever has.

We have all seen the movies where a man looses his wife

and family because he is consumed with his work. He spends no time with them and then one day he comes home to an empty house. Because we see that story on television, we believe that it is common, and no doubt it happens. But I contest that failure ruins more marriages than working too hard. Hard work is a personality trait and any man who has it rarely designates it only to his career. If he works hard at his job, he often works hard keeping his family happy as well. Yes, laziness causes more broken homes compared to hard work.

The self-discovery of business success will grow your relationship with your spouse, your children, your God, and yourself. It is a key part to living well. However, we have a problem. People rarely like self-discovery. We don't really want to know who we are because that allows us to see the ugly side of ourselves. Our ego won't allow us to see clearly who we are because, then, we would have to change. That is really the problem—change.

Of all of the people whom I have helped grow over the years, I can say that my hardest battle has been teaching people the concept of change. Not only is change hard work, which brings out our essence of laziness, it also means admitting we were wrong—and that can be ego shattering.

The second law of thermodynamics informs us that as time progresses, all energy fades into entropy unless acted upon by an outside force. This means that unless energy is introduced to help drive the process, the outcome will become less organized and more chaotic. Energy must be constantly introduced into your life if you wish to progress personally, financially, physically or even socially. If you do nothing in your life, you will not progress. In fact, you will fade into disorganization. You must constantly work on yourself if you wish to expand.

Life does not simply fall into place over time. Time makes us older, slower, weaker and less fit. To ripen as we age, we must continuously work to become quicker, smarter, wiser, and financially wealthy. All aspects of life follow this law and there are no exceptions to God's physical reality.

Because the doctor is the key to success in any office, we have to deal with this idea of self-discovery and the reluctance to change. When a doctor asks me to help them grow their office, one would think that my job would be easy because they have already made the cry for help. But you would be wrong. In general, even the desperate doctor is reluctant to change. Optimistic people look at change as an opportunity to improve, while pessimistic personalities view change in a more fearful manner that may result in life getting worse. Changes in billing, marketing, office staff or documentation is like admitting a wrong. Knowing this about human behavior, I never judge a doctor or consider his or her behavior as wrong. I believe it takes great courage to ask for help. To want a better life for their family and exposing their office to me takes guts. That is why I work hard to give them the results they are looking for.

But, change they must.

Success is a mental sport. In order to get a doctor to the place that I know they can be, I must be their friend, coach, and doctor. I have the daunting task of making them mentally strong, teaching them how to see the pitfalls in their mentality before they become too big, and keeping them in the correct state of mind for business success.

Getting a doctor in the correct mental state may take

many years, however. Neither the doctor nor I have that much time to waste. I have to get instant results. Generally, a doctor is only 90 days from bankruptcy when I am called in to help. On my first encounter with an office, I give them tools and strategies to see a massive, positive growth in 60 to 90 days. Quick fixes are a must, but rarely does a quick fix help over the long term. I will stay with an office on average for 5 years to be their personal coach. This gives me the time to mold the doctor into a lean, mean business machine.

This chapter will be written in the order that I address each problem with the doctor. It is based on what I generally see in the field and what gives our company the quickest results in turning an office around.

Poverty Mentality

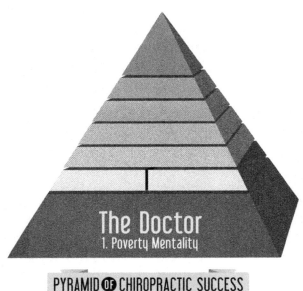

The Doctor
1. Poverty Mentality

PYRAMID OF CHIROPRACTIC SUCCESS

"Money isn't everything but it sure is good."

—Les Brown

This term will be new for many people so first I must explain what I mean by a poverty mentality. Many people look at the world and see only opportunity, love and success. This is not the case for the person with a poverty mentality. They see the world as half empty, while just waiting for the remainder to be lost as well. These are the people who are happy to say, "You can't do that." These doctors feel like they will be audited by the IRS and that the insurance companies are out to get them. They bill small amounts of money to the insurance company because they believe that by billing less, they stay under the radar and will hopefully be left alone.

Many doctors reading this book will be thinking, "I'm not like that. I don't have a poverty mentality." I'm here to tell you that I have never met a person who did not have some degree of a poverty mentality. Sometimes, it shows in their words and other times it shows in their actions, but rest assured, they have it. This is why poverty mentality is the number one problem I see in doctors.

I will give you many examples of how this monster can rear its ugly head and the disaster it can cause. I'm sure that once you see some examples, you will find it in your own life, and practice. I have even been guilty of it from time to time.

Generally, chiropractors come from the lower of the socio-economic classes in America. The majority of your classmates did not come from multiple generations of chiropractors or from affluent families. Sure, there are exceptions, but by and large, it is true. I am happy to say that as more and more chiropractors are becoming successful, that trend is changing. But for now we generally come from families that have little or no money.

Years and years of penny pinching, complaining that things were too expensive, or that they couldn't afford it took root in our minds. The concept that money was scarce and hard to come by consumes our everyday life, until we now act out the behaviors of our parents. Though you have never thought about it, you have to admit that you have heard those statements a lot when you were growing up.

Consider these statements: "Who do you think I am—Donald Trump?"

"Money doesn't grow in trees, you know."

These statements create a deep-rooted disease of the unconscious mind. This disease is reaffirmed every time we struggle over money.

We are proud of our parents, family and upbringing. We can't outright say that our parents were wrong, even though we know we are a product of our environment. This can be a big inner-personal conflict for some people. What you have to realize is that mentality probably served your parents. It helped them cope with the stress of everyday life. It does not serve you.

We must change it if we have any hope of business success. We must kill the monster. We must cure the disease.

Never say, "That's too expensive." If you really desire it say, "Wow. That's nice. I'm going to put that on my goal list and get it someday." Never complain over the lack of money. Get used to quoting Les Brown when he said, "Money isn't everything but it sure is good."

This concept is no hairy, fairy concept. Like the law of attraction, this perspective and manner of speaking is a real solution to a real problem. If you don't think this is applicable to everyday life, let me give you an example.

I have set up many doctors in practice in my life. My favorite thing to do is get doctors straight out of school and set them up. I pay for everything and train them how to be a great chiropractor. I am ashamed to say that I have not done a good job in the past teaching them how to be good business leaders. That is a problem that I have rectified. I guess life is teaching me, too.

I give them a base wage for six months, then 50% of the profits. Once these chiropractors are working for me for three to five years, I give them a buyout option. This is a happy day for the doctors who work for me, because they are going to get a big pay raise overnight. Let me give you a real example. In one office, we were bringing in about $25,000 a month with a low overhead of about $5,000 monthly. That means that, on average, I was getting $10,000 a month from the operation of the office and the doctor working there was getting $10,000 a month. I was prepared to sell it to them for $200,000, which would be a bank note for about $3,000 per month. To make a long story short, the doctor should get an extra $7,000 each month, beginning the moment he buys the office.

The functioning overhead would not change. There is no reason why the patient volume would change, because the patients wouldn't even know the transaction was unfolding. For that reason, the doctor should go from making $120,000 a year to $204,000 a year. I call that a sweet raise.

However, that is not what really happened in this case. The office collections went down, for reasons unknown to me. Maybe the doctor didn't schedule patients for reevaluations maybe he stopped taking X-rays, or maybe he stopped billing properly. I have no idea, and it doesn't matter, because all it tells me is that he has a poverty mentality.

Today he owns the office and is making less than $100,000 a year.

Why would someone sabotage their life like that? Why would someone want less for his or her family? Because, it is human nature. Why does the President of the United States cheat on his wife and loose his social standing? Why would the King of Rock and Roll overdose on drugs? Often, just when it seems like people have it all, they sabotage their life. Are we all destructive deep down inside? Is happiness just a pipe dream that, once attained, still leaves us incomplete? There are parts of me that would like to believe that, but I know many people to the contrary. I know successful, happy people who have a great balance between work, family, and purpose. It does exist.

We all have a self-worth. Some of us believe that we are worth $50,000 a year while others will settle for nothing less than $5,000,000 a year. When we come close to breaking that barrier, we will generally do something to sabotage our growth. To stop the cycle, we first have to realize that it is happening. We have to recognize that there is a destructive part in all of us. We have to transcend it.

Let me give you another example of the poverty mentality that you may see in your own office. It is expected that all offices will have boom times, while other times, income and patient volume is low. What I like to do is plot these numbers on a graph. You can choose any growth category you want over time. Number of patient visits, new patients, collections, billing—anything you want. The longer the time period you use, the more accurate your graph will be. Slight dips are normal. What you want to do is draw an average line and get a general slope of the graph.

If you have an office that is growing over time, it should

have a steady slope to the right, as in figure 3. This is what I would expect to see in any business that is growing. This is the healthy, normal trend of things, and I love to see this graph. This graph tells me that as new patients are coming in, they are referring their friends and family, and therefore, new patient numbers are on the rise, billing is up and therefore, collections are increasing over time.

Figure 3.

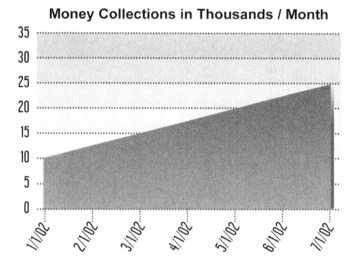

If however, I see a graph like figure 4, I know that there is one of two problems happening. The first, most likely problem, is a poverty mentality where the doctor is content to see a certain number of patients and therefore collect a particular amount of money. When he or she crosses over that threshold of self-worth, the doctor will do something to sabotage success, thus causing the graph to drop. When the levels drop too far and the doctor feels the stress of making too little money, he or she will clean up the act to increase volume, only to repeat the cycle again.

Figure 4.

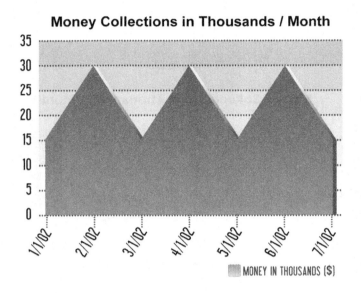

Money Collections in Thousands / Month

MONEY IN THOUSANDS ($)

There are maybe millions of reasons how he or she sabotaged the office: bad scheduling, poor patient education, poor attitude, whatever. When confronted with this information, generally, the doctor will give every reason in the book why it is not his or her fault. They can't see that the problem is them. That is when I know I am in for a struggle. But, I also know that when a breakthrough finally comes, that doctor will be great.

When the physician admits he or she is the problem, my job is so much easier. And the doctor will learn to be great faster.

There is one other reason why a doctor can have a graph like figure 4 with the ups and downs, and that is fatigue. We all have a certain amount of energy that we have to work with in any given day. It is obvious that a doctor has to expend more energy seeing 100 patients per week compared to 40. When the doctor's volume is higher, he or she may feel fatigue or burnout more acutely.

When they exceed their capacity, they will still do something to sabotage their business, but at least it is not due to a poverty mentality. They are doing it now as a protection mechanism to prevent crashing. When the money gets too low, they will get motivated again pick up their energy and start a cycle over again.

If their crossover point is 100 patients per week, I know they have a big problem, because I can see three times that many and not be fatigued. Usually, that means that the doctor has not done anything to recharge his or her life. No vacation, no continuing education, or no time for hobbies to recharge the spirit.

My conversation with them would go something like this. "Every human being is made up more than just the physical body. We have a mental component, a spiritual, emotional, sexual, financial, and many others. These graphs tell me that you have been neglecting at least one of these components in your life." When you are too weighted on one particular area in your life, the rest of you will sabotage another aspect to try and balance yourself. Usually, a vacation takes care of that issue, and they come back ready to grow to the next level.

If, on the other hand, the upper limit is closer to 200 or 300 patients per week, I know that it is time to get an associate.

The doctor is showing the first signs of burnout due to exhaustion. Once we get an associate hired and properly trained, the office will grow again. If the statistics are followed properly, the doctor's business can grow for many years. Plus, he or she can reap the benefits financially as well as knowing the practice has helped possibly millions of people.

This reflects the power of statistics mixed with deductive reasoning. We will talk more about the importance of statistics in the section about business practices.

Remember however, upper limits or fatigue is generally not the reason for the yo-yo quality of figure 4. Usually, it is a poverty mentality. Unless the doctor's thought processes are changed, no skills I teach them will last for the long haul. I can come into his or her office and give a 50% increase in patient volume and a 100% increase in collections. But, within a few months, they will be right back to where they were before I met them. Who you are is reflected in your business, and unless you change who you are, gravity will pull you back down to your old ways. As I said earlier, "Success is a mental game."

I would be lying if I told you that I myself did not deal with this poverty mentality. I am only human, and my demon inside loves to show his face from time to time. I have, however, learned to deal with this evil aspect of human nature better than most. Gay Hendricks' great book, "The Big Leap," deals very well with self-sabotage and discovering one's upper limits of self worth. In the work, he describes how we all have an upper limit to our worth. No matter if we are talking about finances, success, fame, or a loving relationship, we mentally project this upper limit, and will do anything to ensure we stay below this level. When a sports star, movie star, or religious icon becomes too popular, the celebrity frequently will do anything to sabotage his or her social standing.

To them, it is a humbling experience that will equalize their true value. This book is a must read if one is to surmount this negative tendency.

To permanently kill the poverty mentality, you must never feel poor. To kill this thought pattern of feeling poor, we must never complain about not having enough money or be judgmental of how rich people spend their money. If Donald Trump wants to buy a $200 million yacht, I'm happy for him.

It has been said that you must always carry $100 in your pocket, ensuring that you never feel poor. I agree with this in theory. But $100 is not what it used to be. I believe that you should always carry in your pocket as much money as you believe you should make in a day. It is very common to find $2,000 in my pocket. I feel that I'm worth at least that much. That money is not necessarily to spend; it is there to Mentally solidify my self-worth and extinguish the poverty mentality.

There are some who are constantly worried that they will get robbed if they carry that much money, and ask me if it is okay to carry credit cards or debit cards. I know that we have become a credit nation, but, perhaps with the exception of JP Morgan's Chase Palladium card (made of $1,000 of real, 23-karat gold), it is not the same. I don't feel rich having an American Express card or debit card in my pocket. Nothing takes the place of having 20 crisp new $100 bills. If you are concerned about someone stealing or losing your money, it tells me that you don't really believe you are worth the money you carry in your pocket. And what if you lose it? You must learn to adopt a confidence-based feeling of, "Who cares? There is *more* where that came from."

Another way that I work to suppress the poverty mentality is to give money away. I have my favorite charities, and I love to give money to beggars on the street. Your mind truly understands that money is not scarce when you give it away. Like I said before, we must learn to adopt the assurance that "there is more where that came from."

Of course, it can be an ongoing battle to change one's mind and actions. We are a product of decades of programming from our parents, schools and peers. We have been lead to believe that money is hard to come by. But, if you do the right things that I will outline throughout this book, you will see that money is not as hard to come by as you once thought. Reprogramming your mind is no simple task, but it can be done. You just have to work at it—constantly.

Being the Leader

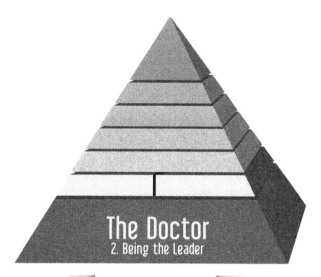

The Doctor
2. Being the Leader

PYRAMID OF CHIROPRACTIC SUCCESS

The true measure of leadership is influence – nothing more, nothing less.

—John C. Maxwell

The second most common problem that I see with doctors struggling to become successful is their lack of leadership. The term leadership has been used so much lately that one hardly even knows what it means anymore. I define leadership, from the chiropractic perspective, as a doctor who has the capacity to persuade and motivate patients and staff to follow what he or she believes to be the correct course of action. Does the doctor exude confidence in ability and therefore demand respect from staff and patients? Does he or she have a knack at getting people to see the bigger picture and outline a course of action that will manifest a desired result?

Authority can be granted based on a person's position in an organization or society. However, mutual respect and true leadership is evident when people will willingly follow you. This respect can never be granted; it must be earned. Leadership authority requires that people respect you in your position of authority, honor your opinion and will follow your direction. Many health care professions have swindled, cheated and convinced the less educated to spend all their money. These unethical practices will never win in the end, but sadly, they have deflated the term "doctor" in the public's eye.

Chiropractors whom I have worked with in the past have often asked, "What makes me qualified to lead these people?" or "What makes me so special that people will follow me?" Both of these statements tell me that the doctor has no true idea of the position he or she holds in the minds of their patients. These doctors will struggle in practice until the day that they recognize their place in the health care arena. Patients come to us feeling lost and without hope. They are looking for assistance and are willing to let you lead them to good health. This position should never be taken lightly.

The fact is, you are special. You went to undergraduate school and then to graduate school, which puts you in the top

2% of America. You have studied hard and have skills that our society desperately needs. You have studied health care, but from an angle not otherwise seen in our society. You can heal the sick without drugs and surgery. If that is not special and unique, then I don't know what is.

Chiropractic leadership should be taught in school. Students graduate with a sense of entitlement that they will get respect from the public because of their degree or title of doctor. Once they are out in practice, they quickly find out that they do not get the respect they think they deserve. Their employer often abuses them, and he or she doesn't seem to care that they have a doctor of chiropractic degree. They can't seem to get patients to listen to their recommendations, and their patient retention as well as patient compliance is horrible. This reality can be deflating. But there are ways to shorten this learning period and improve your odds.

In general, patients come to my office after visiting several other doctors. They have not gotten what they were looking for in my competitors' practices, and so they kept looking. They may have been to many medical doctors, and often to many other chiropractors. What are they searching for? At face value, one would think that they are searching for better health or simply feeling better. To some extent, this is true. But what I believe they are really searching for is a leader. They feel lost and don't know what to do. They have no idea how to improve their health and that is why they are still searching. They want someone to tell them the truth. They want someone to tell them what to do. If they knew what to do, they would already be doing it.

You have to be the one to step up to this task. You have to tell them your finding. You have to make them understand what you will do and what their responsibilities are. No one in the health industry is doing that. Patients are used to getting pills and being told to go home, or they are getting their back "cracked' at another chiropractor's office and told to come back. They have no direction, and when they have no direction, they feel lost.

Patients are looking for a leader to fill this void. If you are the one, they will do anything, within reason, that you ask. But if you are not what they are looking for, they will go somewhere else to continue their search for leadership. No amount of giving away free care or incentives will ever increase your value in the patient's mind. Your value is determined by how easily you are replaced. If the doctor down the road can substitute you, you will have little value in the mind of the patient. Stepping up to your task as the leader makes you irreplaceable.

Most doctors are scared to confront the patient. Getting a patient well requires activity from both the doctor and the patient. It requires passive care, adjustments and active rehabilitation. Most doctors intuitively know this, but are afraid to tell the patient what is needed. If you know that it will take three adjustments for the first two weeks, then tell the patient and schedule them. I have increased a doctor's business by 25% simply by getting them to bulk schedule patients. When you schedule a patient one day at a time, it tells the patient that you have no idea what to expect. The patient figures that any doctor who does not know what to expect must not have good skills. And therefore, the patient will not comply.

I once asked a chiropractor, "Do you think it is better to adjust an acute patient three times a week or two times a week?" She replied, "Three times a week." I had her charts in front of me and I said, "Then, why are you giving your patients inferior care? Most of these patients have been treated one and two times a week." The proof was right in front of her; she could not deny her actions. If you believe that three times per week is better than two times per week, and you don't give your patient the best treatment, then you are an inferior doctor.

Don't be scared to tell patients that you need to see them three times next week. After treating hundreds of patients, a doctor generally knows what outcomes to expect. So, tell the patient, and you will see that compliance is much greater.

Next, it is always better to over treat a patient than under treat. It strokes my ego when I get a patient well before expected but I can't rely on the rare few that fall out of statistical norms.

I have had hundreds, maybe thousands, of patients who have come to me looking for help after they have already been to another chiropractor. They always give me a reason why they thought it was necessary to make the switch, but mainly, it is because they were not getting well at the other office. Do you think they say, "I was treated 25 times at the other doctor's office and didn't get well," or do you think they say, "I was treated for four months by the other doctor and didn't get well?" In other words, do you think they refer to number of treatments they had or length of time they went to the other chiropractor? I can assure you that 90% or more use time as their guiding factor.

Let me give you this scenario. Let's assume that the other doctor was treating a patient once every two weeks for four months, which would be eight visits, and never got them well. Do you believe that is a reflection of the other doctor's skill as a chiropractor, or a reflection of his lack of leadership skills? I feel the other doctor could have easily gotten my new patient well if only he stepped up to the task of treating the patient frequently. Very few patients are well after eight visits in my office, especially if they are spaced by two weeks. Patients will give you a window of time. Use it wisely.

I did an exam, X-rays and told the patient, in their terms, what was wrong and what had to be done to fix their ailment. I scheduled them 3 times a week for the first week and told them I would reevaluate on Friday. If they improved, I would decrease their frequency the following week, but if I did not see the improvement I wanted, I would see them three times the following week as well. Nobody ever questions my authority when it comes to managing patients. In four weeks, that patient was feeling much better and already referred three others to my office.

You need to understand that every patient you have is going to be talking about you around the dinner table whether you want them to or not. You have the ability to determine if your name is used favorably or not. If you don't get them well, they will publicize it to everyone they know. But, equally, if you *do* get them well, they will also spread the good news. Your choice! Schedule your patients properly and get them well.

Within the topic of leadership, we also need to talk about your ability to keep patients motivated. The day they walk into your office, they are extremely motivated by pain. As the pain drifts away, even minimally, they will want to quit their treatment. We all know if they quit, their pain will return, because the problem was not really fixed. The patient will still hurt and they will not be raving fans. They will still talk about you to their family and friends, but it will not be as favorable as if their pain was gone and their function was returned to normal.

I can hear the conversations go something like this: A friend asks, "How is your treatment going with that chiropractor you are seeing?"

"Not bad," the patient replies. "I feel some better, but my back still hurts."

"Who was it you were seeing?" the nosy friend wants to know.

And now you have lost. Your name will not be associated with success with this possible patient, or worse, this potential patient simply believes that chiropractic, as a whole, is just not that effective.

No, your educational job is not done when you get the patient in the door. You have to be constantly motivating them to stay the course and see the treatment plan through. Motivation however, is a slippery slope. Not everybody can motivate people. One needs first to be seen as a picture of integrity. The patient must trust you and must never get the feeling you want them to return to line your pockets with money.

To fill the proper role in a patient's mind, you have to be genuine, caring, and be concerned with multiple aspects of their life, not just their chiropractic problems. You must be a fountain of knowledge for your patients, and you must learn the art of effective communication. This is a topic that I will talk more about later.

It goes without saying that you should always be genuine and caring, but many chiropractors believe that you must never get into other issues with your patients other than their chiropractic problems. I do not believe that is the way of a caring doctor. I have had patients cry on my shoulder about losing a loved one or losing a job. They tell me their darkest secrets all because they trust me, and they know I am caring. When you are on that level with a patient, they could never be stolen by another doctor giving away free X-rays and 10 free adjustments. Become a part of their life, and you will brand yourself forever.

When they trust you, they will ask your opinion about everything from medications they are taking, nutritional products and even financial education. Be careful not to overstep your boundaries. But I find it is fine to tell them your opinion as long as you tell them it is just your opinion, not necessarily fact. Become a fountain of knowledge and you will fill this gap in their life, which is just one more way to keep that patient forever.

The proper sequence for service is simple: BE. DO. HAVE. One should never expect to have a growing, thriving, prosperous business without first being what people want you to be. You must then show integrity by practicing what you preach. Be the picture of health and get adjusted often. Only then will you have the life you want. Nothing in this world is free; you must earn what you have.

Be it! Do it! Then have it!

Support Team

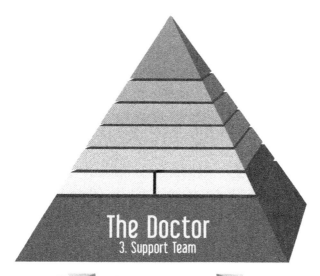

The Doctor
3. Support Team

PYRAMID **OF** CHIROPRACTIC SUCCESS

"Two are better than one, because together they can work more effectively. If one of them falls down, the other can help him up... Two people can resist an attack that would defeat one person alone. A rope made of three cords is hard to break."

—Ecclesiastes 4:9

I have a full section later in this book about staff. That is not what I am talking about when I say support team. This is the third biggest deficit, and a major problem I see when assisting struggling doctors. No man is an island, and no one can stay motivated for long without the loving support of family and friends.

When I interview a potential doctor who wants my help, I insist that their spouse be present for some portion of the process. I have learned the hard way that no one can succeed if they are being constantly bombarded with negativity at home. I am not a marriage counselor, and I would never suggest that a doctor divorce a spouse. So I simply will not coach a doctor or take them under my wing once I discover the doctor has a negative influence at home. There is no amount of work that I do with a doctor that can withstand the negative onslaught of the spouse. Their negative influence completely negates my positive. I cannot be with the doctor 24/7, and therefore I can't win.

I have tried in the past to assist a doctor who had a negative wife, and I quickly discovered that I could not win. The sad thing is that his wife was mainly negative about the money he was not making, and that is what I was there to help with. I could have helped their marriage so much, too. All I needed was time, but every time I got a piece of the doctor's mind, he would come to our next meeting deflated by his wife. It is a sad situation, but I had to get out before I got sucked into this black hole. The last I heard, that doctor was bankrupt financially, and from what I could tell, emotionally bankrupt as well.

It has been said, "Behind every great man, there is a great woman." Even though that statement seems sexist, I know the genders can be reversed. I know I could not be anywhere nearly as successful as I am today without the loving support of my wife. Two minds are better than one, and it is easier to endure the hardships that are bound to come your way if you have a supportive team on your side. It is an absolute must that a doctor has a support team if they expect to succeed.

At times, the negative influence in a doctor's life is not the spouse, but a friend, mother-in-law, father, or someone else in the family. It is much easier to eliminate or limit these people's influence in your life, if you must, than it is to eliminate a spouse. Sometimes, it is as simple as not going to the mother-in-law's house for Sunday dinner.

I will, however, take on a client that has a negative influence that is not the spouse. I am such a positive influence that I can usually negate the negativity of someone they do not have to face on a daily basis. Results however, are much greater and faster when all negative influence is taken away from the doctor. So my advice to you is to eliminate all negative people from your life.

We do live in a negative world, and if you fall into that negativity, you will struggle. In the book, "The Magic Story," Frederick Van Rensselaer Dey stated, "Life has many pathways, and of them, by far the greater number lead downward." Without constantly feeding your mind, and associating with positive people, your pathway will also lead down. To propel your life up, you have to surround yourself with the right associates. Your family and your friends should be your biggest allies. They must recognize when you are becoming negative and that your life is turning to the dark side. They must assist you in turning your attitude around.

If you have these people in your life, you are in luck. Do your best to love them for the gifts they really are. If you do not have people of this caliber in your life, you must find them, or struggling will become your prison forever.

In addition to having the right people in your life, you must also feed your mind with the proper motivational material, which is the topic of our next section.

Motivation

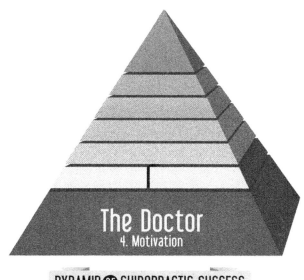

PYRAMID **OF** CHIROPRACTIC SUCCESS

"Love is a greater motivator than duty."

—Albert Einstein

The role we play every day is not an easy one. There are times that I wonder if it is all worthwhile. Luckily, that is not very often. I am generally very happy with my choice in career, but I will be the first to say that there are easier ways to make a living.

To persevere in this profession, you must have some deep motivation. I use the term motivation here in what I believe, maybe, is the wrong context, but I do that on purpose. What I would have rather stated is that you must have a strong WHY. However, I knew that I would have been completely misunderstood had I written that first.

I see the art of motivation and motivational speaking as a very temporal thing. It is easy to be motivated one minute and the next, find yourself in the doldrums of despair. In that light, motivation is not what we really need to sustain us through the hard times. No, what we really need is something that is unwavering, constant and something we can always count on. I call that your WHY.

Why do you get up in the morning and get a shower? Why do you go to work? Why do you run your own business? Why did you get married? Why do you see all those patients? Why do you bill insurance? Why do you do all that paper work?

A doctor must have a big enough WHY or he or she will feel like their life is dull and pointless. This is the reason motivation is placed as the fourth biggest problem I see inhibiting the success of doctors.

The topic of motivation can be difficult. I have always said that I like dealing with clients and staff motivated by money and business success, because that is usually something that I can help them with. These are people that I understand and relate to, and for that reason, it is easier for me to get inside their mind. If you are motivated more by family values, you may need a different coach. This is not to say that family is not important. In fact, it is one of the most important things in my life. However, there are people out there who can help you who are more qualified than me.

What motivates one person may not motivate the next. It can be, at times, the search for the proverbial needle in the haystack. But, search we must, and we have to determine your why if we have any hopes of finding adequate fuel for your success.

It has been said that we crave and are on a quest only for the things that we don't already possess. This statement seems trivial, but there is a lot of wisdom in those few words. Only the poor are on the constant quest for money. If you are searching for love in your life, it is only because you have interpreted that you don't already have it. Likewise, doctors searching for the magic secret to success are doing so only because they believe they are not already there.

I can better determine a client's WHY as I discover his or her cravings. Are they longing to take their family on a trip to Hawaii? Are they dreaming of a new sports car or yacht? The answers to these questions give me a glimpse into my client's mind so I can motivate them correctly.

As I stated earlier, motivation is temporal. It is a common occurrence to see a doctor's patient volume and collections skyrocket after a motivationally or clinically relevant seminar, only to see the boost fade back to normal after a month or two. I would even guess that you will see a boost in your business after reading this book. But, as the weeks pass, you will drift down to your normal patient and collections level because your energy, enthusiasm, and passion will wane.

It will not last. Motivation is not enough to sustain you through the tough times. To sustain your office and your life, you must determine your WHY.

Einstein, Gandhi, and Nelson Mandela all knew their WHY. They have all endured great hardship and persevered. There is no way to accomplish what they did with motivation alone. They had a purpose that they felt was greater than themselves and that gave them the strength to carry on. They will be remembered for eternity for their work, and so could you.

It took me my whole life to discover my WHY, and my unique gifts. In many ways, I am still developing my answer. But, not until I discovered why God placed me on this planet, at this particular time, did I blossom into the person I am today. Prior to this time, I was constantly looking for external motivation. I have seen way more motivational speakers than I care to admit. Like you, I got a boost in my financial life each time I returned from those seminars. And in that way, they were really helpful, but there was no end to it. Now that I have found my purpose, my office is booming all of the time.

Generally, when I ask a person to tell me their WHY, I get prefabricated answers that lack the necessary substance. This proves to me they are still searching, and that is a good thing. However, standard answers to these deeper questions will not aid us in our struggles. It feels more like small talk about the weather than the profound purpose to one's existence. Prefabricated statements mean they are only telling me what I want to hear, or they are telling me someone else's story.

These are personal questions and cannot be answered without deep reflection. Writer and Nobel Prize winner Andre Gide once said, "It is better to fail at your own life than to succeed at someone else's." Life is too short to live any life but your own.

We all have to find a deeper meaning to our existence. God placed us here for a reason, and it is up to us to determine that reason. When you embrace that discovery, your life will flow the way it is meant to. Once we find this deeper, internal WHY, we will no longer need to be motivated externally. However, it may take my clients years to discover this purpose. So until that time, I do everything I can to keep them motivated. It is not ideal, but it is all we have.

Once I accept a client, I provide them with all of the motivational books and CDs I want them to listen to. I have a collection of favorite motivational material that I give in a particular sequence to aid them on their path to success. I have found that these materials can dramatically increase a doctor's volume and income in a short time.

I am amazed at how many people, including doctors, don't read. I ask them to read motivational books and educational material, and all I hear is a sigh of disbelief that I am actually asking them to read. Many doctors thought they could give up reading and studying as soon as they graduated. I'm sorry, my friend. The quest must go on.

There is a commitment that you must make when you decide to be a successful doctor. You have to continuously read to stay motivated and to stay educated.

"My uncle is very successful, and he hardly reads at all," I hear one student proclaim. I usually reply by saying, "My grandfather smoked a pack of cigarettes a day for 75 years and is still alive. That doesn't mean that it is a smart thing to do."

No matter where you look, there are people defying the odds. Sure, you can become successful without reading, but I have decided to play better odds. I once heard that the average millionaire in America reads 17 books a year, 15 of which are non-fiction. If you want to be a millionaire, mimic millionaires, and if you want to be a failure, mimic failures. Besides, if you don't read, you might as well not know how to read. What is the function of a skill that is not utilized?

Improving the Doctor's Communication

PYRAMID **OF** CHIROPRACTIC SUCCESS

"The problem is not so much of communication. It is identification."

—Charlie "Tremendous" Jones

Patients and staff are not mind readers. The only way to lead is through effective communication. Proper communication is an art form, and just like any other art, it can be learned. It does come easier for some people, but that is not to say anybody can't learn.

We have all been in enough arguments with family, friends or customer service representatives to experience the age-old problem with debating. At times, it seems as though we can say anything we want and the other party just can't seem to get it. We wonder if they are even listening, or maybe it is because they are just not as smart as us.

You know what I mean. You feel as if you are talking to a wall and nothing is getting accomplished. This is the best example of ineffective communication. If you are having many of these conversations, there is no way you can lead.

To prevent this infinity loop of ineffective conversation, we must first identify with the other individual. You must know what they desire out of the conversation, and you must know from what perspective they are coming from. This requires a person to listen first and talk last.

This sequence sounds easy enough, but is harder than you might expect. I have been caught making the faux pas many times before I learned this important distinction. I actually had one person say to me, "Are you really listening to what I have to say, or are you simply waiting for your turn to speak?" The truth of that statement stung, but it only brought to the surface something I knew I was guilty of.

When the person you are wishing to have a conversation with feels that you understand them, they are in the proper mental position to listen to your words. Prior to that point, you are wasting your breath. Connecting with your patients or staff will allow you to lead them more effectively.

Also, connecting to people is much simpler when you have a genuine love for others and you sincerely want to connect. It can be accomplished simply by asking a person what an ideal outcome would be. Sitting in a chair next to them as an equal rather than towering over them, looking them in the eye as you speak, nodding appropriately to their words, and asking for greater clarification from them at important junctures all allow you to connect with a person. It shows them that you care and relate to them. At this point, you are ready to make recommendations or demands. By now, generally the person will do whatever you want them to do, within reason.

Parents relate to other parents. Farmers relate to other farmers. When people relate to others, they will tell them anything they want to know. But if patients don't relate to their doctor, the physician has lost before he or she has even started. Spend the time and effort to relate to people before you communicate, and you will soon find out that your life will be much easier. Try and skip this step, and you will talk all day to a person and get nowhere.

I am not a lover of scripted conversations. Many doctor's offices use scripted conversations because they feel it standardizes the process and cuts down on confusion. Scripts remove a person's personality and natural charm from the conversation, and I feel patients would rather talk to a genuine, loving person.

There are times when scripts are a good idea. It amazes me that even though we live in an insurance world, there are patients who still don't understand terms like copay and deductibles. Our staff used to tell patients that they have a $20 copay and a $250 deductible and just leave it at that.

But then, we would have so many irate patients after they received a bill stating they were unaware they had to pay that amount of money.

Because I hate the concept of hidden fees, we had to rectify this situation. Once we discovered that it was a terminology problem, I insisted my secretaries improve their conversations to something like this: "Mrs. Smith, you have a $250 deductible, which means you have to pay $250 before your insurance will pay anything. And you also have a $20 copay, meaning you will have to pay us $20 before each visit with the doctor. Do you understand what your insurance policy demands of you?"

Rather than simply using the terms with patients, my staff *defines* the terms to eliminate any possible confusion. Is this a scripted conversation? I would say NO. It is effective conversation. My employees are still free to add their own flair to the conversation, allowing it to be genuine.

Once patients are back in the treatment room, they need to feel your concern, your confidence, your skill, your understanding, and they are in the right place to get their problems fixed. Generally, most patients have been to many other doctors before coming to your office. To many patients, chiropractic is still looked at as alternative care, or, to some, as quackery. So they are stepping out of their comfort zone coming to you. They have had little success getting well with other professions, and what they are really looking for is hope and the sense that they are in the correct place. How do they know they are in the right place? Tell them!

Once I do my initial assessment and determine that I can help them, I make it a point to tell my patients they came to the right place. It gives them a sense of relief and hope. My conversation is not scripted, but will go something like this: "Mrs. Jones, I sense your concern about being here for your hip pain. I know that you are scared and concerned that you are not in the right place. I have done an exam and studied your X-rays. I have found the reason why you are having pain, and I can tell you that you are in the right place. Because I want to earn your trust and respect, I want to be straightforward with you, right from the start.

"Your problem is complex, and that is probably why other doctors have had little success treating you. I have treated many patients with similar problems. And it will not be easy to get you well, but I can tell you I have gotten many people with your problem to feel great. I will work with you using all my skill, passion and knowledge, as I do with all my patients, to get you feeling better."

There are many aspects of the above conversation that will assist me in leading and managing this patient. I first justified her concerns of being in the correct place for her problem. Next, I told her I did an in-depth study, and finally found what was wrong, and that gave her confidence in my ability. Then, I told her that she was in the correct place. Third, I set the stage for a candid relationship based on mutual respect.

Next, patients usually feel that their problem is unique and more severe than anyone realizes. So, by telling her that her problem was complex and difficult, I justified in her mind that I truly acknowledge and believe the suffering she is experiencing. Then, lastly, I tell her that I will do anything within my power to see she gets well, which now makes us team members in the fight to improve her condition.

The above conversation would have been useless unless I had the right eye contact, and tone. More than words are needed to have an effective conversation. Most importantly of all, this conversation told Mrs. Jones, unconsciously, that I related to her struggle. We have established a rapport that as long as I deliver my promises to get her well, she will be a patient forever.

People don't cheat on their family. And now I am a part of her family, and she cannot be enticed away by cheaper service. Develop the rapport, and you can grow an office very fast. Fail to do it, and you will have a long career of a frustrating search for new patients.

In essence, to have effective conversations, you must know something about human psychology. People have a deep need to be right, appreciated, and understood. Ask yourself: What am I currently doing to make patients feel that way?

"You will get all that you want as long as you help enough people get what they want."
—Zig Ziglar

The art of effective communication can be used in any social situation. With your spouse, your kids, friends, or coworkers. People would like to think that they make decisions logically, and that they don't make them emotionally. Actually, they usually make decisions based on how it makes them feel.

By making someone else feel significant, understood, loved, and appreciated, you can have more effective conversations. Conversations that have outcomes that are more in line with what you want.

But one cannot gain rapport with all people using the same questions. It is illogical to think that a 45-year-old, stay-at-home mom can be related to on the same level as a 55-year-old, male steel worker. To gain rapport, you first have to know something about the individual. People love to talk about themselves, and you have to allow them to fulfill that desire. If you let people talk, most times they will tell you what is needed to relate to them.

If you have no idea where to start with a patient, you can start by asking them to describe their average day. They will believe that you are doing this to determine what they may be doing at work or at home to aggravate their condition. You *are* doing it for that reason, but also, you are doing it for a much grander purpose. You are trying to see what it will take to relate to them. How can you get on their level? What key words will they spill allowing you to meet on common ground? It could be cooking, working, taking care of kids, nutrition, or anything else. If you let them talk, you will find that which binds us all.

A word of important caution here: I do not do this in a manipulative way. Mental manipulation is not in my person-ality. I do it because I would love to have a real relationship with everyone I meet. I want to relate to everyone, so we can have more than just small talk. Deep conversations are rare because most people don't take the time to really get to know someone. Getting on a deeper level with more people increases everyone's quality of life, including yours.

I read this poem years ago, and it summarizes exactly how I feel about communication. But I have to apologize, be-cause I do not know the author, and an online search came up empty. Effective communication is one of the most important elements in life—not just with your patients, but also your employees, family and friends.

What I get to say is not what I want to say.
It is not what they listen to.
It is not what they hear.
It is what they understand.
What do I want them to remember when I'm gone?
I need to say that, and only that.
Clearly

Changing the Doctor's Mental State

The Doctor
6. Changing the Doctor's State

PYRAMID OF CHIROPRACTIC SUCCESS

"Nothing can be changed without first changing state."
—Anthony Robbins

Change is difficult, even when you know it's necessary. One of the key things that I do when I take on a client is show them the necessity of change. My philosophy is that success is a collection of habits and procedures that are repeated until you get the desired outcome. Failure is equally a set of habits that lead down a less desirable path. When I tell clients my philosophy, they quickly agree. Agreement, however, is easy until I show them many of their failure habits, and tell them they have to change.

People do not like to change. They want to keep doing what they are doing and expect things to get better. I'm here to tell you that will rarely happen. We have to change if we want our dreams to come true. But, as Anthony Robbins says, we first have to change our state.

Your current state of mind has gotten you where you are today. Nobody would hire me to keep them where they are. They hire me to get them to where they want to be, and that requires change. First, a change of state, then a change of action.

Right about here is when our topic gets a little metaphysical. I'm sure you have all noticed that when you are in a great mood, and things are going great, they seem to continue to get great. Yet, when things are bad and you are in a sour mood, your patients call and cancel and things seem to go wrong. This is not some mysterious coincidence. That's the way the universe works.

You cannot afford to allow that state of mind to hinder your success. The problem, however, is that we are reactors to our life. If the sun is shining and everything goes fine at home or office, we are in a good mood. But, when the rain is falling and you get wet getting out of your car, you stub your toe on the coffee table, and your spouse was in one of those moods this morning, your outlook sucks.

You are simply reacting to the environment, and therefore,

you are not controlling your life. You are a slave to the external world. To get your life and your practice to the next level, you have to transcend that behavior. You must be the setter of moods, *not* the reactor. You must act consciously to bring light where there is darkness. Be that person, and people will be drawn to you. Act unconsciously, and you will have an office that experiences constant ups and downs.

I am not a robot, and I have to admit there are times that I can't seem to control my moods. But those days are much rarer than they used to be. I have more days where I feel like I am in the zone, compared to days that suck. My patients constantly call me the happiest man they know. The reason I am the happiest man in the world is that I know I'm in control of my thoughts and moods. Good thoughts mean good moods. Bad thoughts mean bad moods. It's that simple.

Keep your mind focused on the way you want things to be and the world will deliver. Focus your mind on the mental picture of success, happiness, prosperity, and love. Then and only then will you be creating your reality.

Let me give you a real world example that we may all be able to relate to. Back in high school, most of us played some type of team sport or we were affiliated with a sport in some manner. Did you ever notice that when you were playing against a team that was relatively equally matched, the game seemed to flip flop from one team winning to the other. Did you ever notice why? One team would come out on the field with more positive energy than the other, and they quickly would dominate. Then, something would happen. Someone on the other team would score or someone on your team would make a simple mistake, resulting in the other team taking the lead.

As energies would swing back and forth between teams, so would the score. Whoever was the most passionate and positive about success would be winning. What does that tell us? That when all things are equal, the person, or team, that has the best attitude rises to the top.

I want the readers of this book to rise to the top. The only way to do that is for you to realize that it is you who are in control. If you want a better outcome, pick a better mood, or better state.

It has been said that in order to fix a problem, you must first admit that you have one. I hope that at this juncture I have gotten you to admit that you have a problem and the problem is YOU. Now that we have come this far, the next step it to learn how to fix it.

The first step to keeping you in the proper state is to teach you how to get into the proper state. This is how I love to do it. During lectures, I usually tell the audience to close their eyes to visualize what it is that I am about to say, but obviously, you can't read with your eyes closed. So please read the following words and then close your eyes and repeat the sequence in your mind. The repetition would be good for you, anyway.

Imagine walking into your office in the morning and being greeted by your secretary stating that you have a call from one of your patients. Let's call her Betty. You have no idea what to expect. At first you think that there is something seriously wrong with Betty. She has never called you in the morning before. So naturally you think the worse. (Which is the tendency of most minds.)

You answer the phone with an apprehensive, "Hello, this is Dr. Smith. How can I help you?" At this point, your patient goes on to tell you that she could not stop thinking about you this morning and felt that she had to call you. She goes on to say, "I just wanted to call and let you know that I have been coming in to see you now for over three years. You have taken care of all of my family—my husband, my children and I want to let you know how much you mean to us. Your skill and love that you show to our family tells me that you are truly one of God's gifts to the world. I just wanted to call you and tell you that I hope you live a long life so you can show as many people as possible the love you have shown us. God bless you, and I will see you next month."

As I said earlier, I now want you to close your eyes and visualize that scenario happening to you. Think as descriptively as you can. Think about the smell and the feel of your office, and even the texture of the phone next to your face. Now, think about how that call would make you feel. Do not rush this procedure. Take as long a time as you need to get as much out of the mental state.

Who would say that for the rest of the day you would be a better doctor? Who thinks that they would have more success? Who believes that they would attract more new patients? Have fewer missed appointments? Who thinks their mood would be better than it has been in weeks? Who believes you would be a better spouse, father, mother, boyfriend, or girlfriend? Do you think you would be a better communicator? Deliver a better chiropractic adjustment?

Most everyone who has done this exercise believes that they would be better in all areas of their life after a call from Betty. But, Betty didn't teach you how to be a better doctor. She did not show you how to attract more patients, deliver a better adjustment or be a better spouse. However, her words did all those things and more. Why?

Because it changed your mood! It changed your belief systems and it gave you a larger sense of self-worth. In essence, it changed your mental state. You felt unstoppable and in the zone simply because Betty told you. Or, better yet, Betty gave you permission. Betty is not an authority on what makes a great doctor. But, we trust her because she flattered us. We all love to be flattered.

I once heard Zig Ziglar reenact a scenario similar to the above example. I just simply made mine chiropractic. I was amazed at the clarity that it gave me about the workings of the human mind, and how easily we can change our day around. A successful life is nothing more than a constant string of successful days. If we can learn the art of changing our mental state, we can have the success we all have dreamed of.

The above example is very effective, but it can be time consuming. So I find that it is important to find a more rapid way to alter our crappy moods. Once you internalize the value in altering your moods, you will get better at recognizing when you are starting to slip to the negative side. Once you see yourself slip, you have to quickly change it.

I believe that music is one of the best ways to quickly alter your mood. I tell patients all the time to make a CD of their favorite music they listened to when they were a teenager or young adult. This is not just any music, but the music they listened to when they felt like they could take on the world. Dance music, heavy metal, or the music they loved to sing into their hairbrush. Choose music that, if you were listening to now, would be an instant cure for depression. Once they get the CD made, they have to put it in their car and never listen to it unless they feel themselves slipping into a negative state. Then, they are permitted to take it out and play it as loudly as they want.

This procedure can alter a mental state in less than five minutes. It will make you feel powerful, young, energetic, and optimistic. Learn to capitalize on these moods to your advantage.

Another quick way to alter mental state is via visualizations. The question is: What do you visualize? If I am anxious, I visualize standing in a beautiful stream, trout fishing with a fly rod. I feel the cold water through my waders and hear the blend of birds chirping mixed with slow, running water. Before you know it, my anxious feeling is gone.

If my office is not feeling successful, I visualize my office waiting room full of people. Patients coming in on time, people happy, people paying their bill, people referring other patients. I picture in my mind all of the good stories they are telling their friends on how I changed their life. I know that it is my purpose to serve humanity in this way, so I feel God's purpose flowing through me. This feeling removes all doubt, destroys the poverty mentality, and welcomes the prosperity one should expect with supplying your talents to the world.

To maintain this mental state over the long haul, it is necessary to reward yourself for reaching your goals. Your mind is an organ like all others, and if you don't give it what it deserves, it will not stand the test of time. Determine what it is that you need to feel rewarded. It is important you feel that the fruits of your labor have been worth the struggle. Some people love to travel and it rejuvenates their soul. Some love to go hiking in the woods, go camping, or fishing, and after such a trip, they come back to the office with new vigor. Some love to drive cars while others love to ride horses. We are not all made the same, and we are all not stimulated or rejuvenated by the same things. Learn what it is that you need and supply it as frequently as you can.

You cannot afford to have one miserable day in your office, if you can prevent it. That one day will act like a cancer and ruin a week or possibly a month. I tell my associates that if you are a parasite or a mental weakling compared to your patients, then God will not put his children in your office. You have to have a healing mentality, which means that you have to have an energy that is better, stronger or healthier than the people you are trying to help. Otherwise, you will be bringing them down. If you can't uplift them, God will protect them, and keep them away from your diseased state.

I know these are powerful words, but I have proven the truth in this statement many times. Sadly enough, I have lost hundreds of thousands of dollars learning this lesson. I can no longer afford to be in a bad mental state, and neither can you. So reward yourself for the attainment of your goals. It will keep you in the proper mental state to heal the world, one patient at a time.

We live in a negative world. We are constantly bombarded with negativity in the news and from everyone around us. There are only a few paths that lead to success, but many that lead to failure. We have to constantly be putting in positive energy and working on ourselves to keep our mental state high. Otherwise, it will naturally gravitate down.

Keep feeding your mind on things that motivate you and

inspire you, in the quest to keep you on track. This is one of the main reasons to determine your WHY, as was discussed earlier in this book. In addition, you must also shelter yourself from the negative. I don't suggest that you be naive to the world's struggles, but too much negativity without the power to change it results in a sense of learned helplessness, which is one of the worst mental states in which to keep oneself.

I seldom listen to the radio, read the newspaper, or watch too much news on television. I am aware of the wars or a famine going on somewhere on this planet, but what good does my negativity add to the situation. I keep my mind elevated, happy, fresh, prosperous, and generous.

Changing your mental state for the long term is a full-time job. But, believe me, it gets easier. I now rarely criticize, complain, judge, or be in a sour mood, and that has made all of my work pay off. The four main things that I have learned to keep my mind in the proper place are as follows.

1) Feed your mind daily with motivational and inspirational books and CDs.
2) Read your short- and long-term goals every day.
3) Create and read out loud daily affirmations on how your day will unfold and the good that you will perform in this world.
4) Keep company with positive people who make you grow and feel good about yourself, while keeping your distance from negative influences.

The Doctor's Integrity

"If you want to be successful, you have to take 100% responsibility for everything you experience in your life."
—Jack Canfield

There are many definitions of integrity. All the definitions, however, speak of being true to yourself, practicing what you preach, and following through with your promises.

As I mature, I see this integrity trait dwindling in our

society. We have reached a point where professionals who are in the market to sell their services don't seem too excited about being successful at selling their services. Who has not called a plumber to fix a leak, heard him promise to be there at 3 p.m., only to leave you sitting around waiting? Eventually, you call him and he states that something came up and he can't make it. You somehow called his phone but he could not call yours. We wait and feel lied to by the cable man, the phone repair guy, the electrician, and even your medical doctor.

It is so common that we have learned to expect it. We expect our medical doctor to be an hour or more behind schedule. We expect to call the repair guy maybe two or three times before he actually finishes the work. Business has regressed to mediocre service and mediocre integrity. In days gone by, when money was scarce, business was all about what they could do for me, but now they act as if they are doing me a favor. It is difficult to know whom you can count on.

However, I see opportunity in this business mess. All you have to do is be the opposite. A business that shows a little integrity shines like a new penny. A diamond business will stand out in the coal dust; we are easily recognized and quickly appreciated by our customers. You can be such an oddity that standing out in a crowd is not hard because the only thing you are doing is acting the way you really are.

I am on time in my office. I do what I say I'm going to do. I don't make promises that I can't keep and I treat my patients with the God-given respect they deserve. No lies, no hidden charges, no mental manipulation and no guilt. Patients feel loved and appreciated in my office, and that is why I feel like family to them and that is also why they keep coming back.

Of course, over the years, I have lost a few patients to other chiropractors in my area. But they always seem to come back with a pocket full of interesting stories from the other doctors' offices. I have heard so much garbage that at times I am embarrassed by what happens in some chiropractic offices.

The doctor being behind an hour is the least of their worries. I have heard of front office staff calling an ex-wife to tell her that her former husband pays his tab with $100 bills. I have heard chiropractors tell patients to stop taking life-giving medication because their adjustment or their vitamins they sell would cure them. The patients complied and ended up in the hospital and nearly died.

Don't be that doctor who leads people down false avenues or promises them the world that you can't deliver. You show a lack of integrity when you do those things. It not only hurts you; it hurts the profession.

What have you promised your patients but are not fulfilling? Did you tell them you would give them exercises in three weeks but forgot to do it? Did you make an appointment for them, but you were an hour behind? Did you promise them to try your best to get them well but all you have done is give them the same adjustment every time they came in?

Where are you lying to your patients? You can't get away with it. This could be the reason you are constantly looking for new patients, can't keep existing patients, or are not getting referrals.

Everything that you say and do is a reflection of your personality. We are all in a constant state of self-definition. Ralph

Waldo Emerson is quoted as saying, "What you do speaks so loud that I cannot hear what you say." You cannot hide your personality from people. You are constantly being judged by the world we live in. Speak and act how you would like to be perceived. If you want to be perceived as a surfer dude then act and speak like a surfer dude. But if you want to be respected and perceived like a doctor, than act and speak like a doctor.

In my definition of integrity, we also have to be true to ourselves. To illustrate the value of being true to oneself, I created the integrity circle.

Figure 5.
The Integrity Circle

The integrity circle illustrated in figure 5 was created to

help you determine who you really are and learn to be true to your nature. It is a way of living more congruently. It is based on the presupposition that you are either attracting people into your life or you are repelling them. Darkness cannot exist in the presence of light and you cannot be inside and outside at the same time. The relative terms do not allow you to play both fields. They are considered mutually exclusive.

Until you discover who you are, it would be wise to take what I am about to describe to you to the nth degree. I take this method to the extreme. It helps me determine what car to drive, what clothes to wear and what books to read.

Let me explain it this way. If I read a book that is not congruent with who I am, I tend to find that the number of patients that I am seeing in my office while I am reading that book tends to decrease, sometimes dramatically. Normally, people are not looking at the correlation between what they are reading and their business success, so instead, they look for other reasons. There is a recession, the kids are on spring break, it's just before Christmas, or it is just after Christmas.

But, really, it could just be that you are engaged in a process of reading something that takes away from who you are rather than adding to you.

The reverse can also be seen, of course. At times, I read a book that inspires me and new patients seem to come out of the woodwork. The book is more in line with my authentic self and therefore, I attract people.

I once drove my wife's BMW sports car back and forth to work for two weeks, and noticed that I had one of the worst two-week patient volumes in my whole career. I start to drive my Mercedes SUV again and my numbers came back to normal. Is it a coincidence? Maybe. But, why would I care? I dare not test my driving experience again. There is too much at stake. I have a successful life to live and as you recall me saying earlier, "A successful life is a collection of successful days." I have no days to spare, so I take it seriously.

Figure 5 illustrates the integrity circle. The center of the integrity circle represents you in your concentrated, ideal form. It is you on your best day. It is what you should hope to be at all times. Each spoke on the integrity wheel represents an aspect of your life. The car you drive, the books you read, your wife, your husband and the million other aspects that make you who you are. Some spokes take you further away from your true self, while others lead you to your authentic self. When we are authentic, people are attracted to us, and when we are phonies, people are repelled by us.

By quantifying the number of people in our life, we can accurately gauge who we are and if we are being true to our nature.

I personally attempt to be as detailed as possible about using the integrity circle. Success lies in the details, and these details help me better understand myself. We are all on a path of self-discovery, and this tool aids us in this discovery.

One cannot finish the topic of integrity without tackling the depth of a person's commitment. How committed to success are you? Many would look me boldly in the face and tell me they are committed to the end—but probably would not do the work and self-refinement necessary to succeed in the chiropractic profession. Life is not a game!

As far as we know, you will get only one shot at our life on this planet. It is not a game that can be restarted. You as the doctor have to realize that by attending school to be the doctor, you have committed yourself to become a success. Your oath to yourself is important—as important as your marriage vows.

Divorce rates are so high because few really realize what it is like to stick with something and make it work. It is not going to be easy. Who lied to you and told you that it was going to be easy? Who lied to you and told you that becoming a successful chiropractor was going to be easy? Successful living is reserved only for the people who have proved their worthiness. Have you put in the work, the energy, the motivation and the commitment to earn the title doctor? Have you put in the effort to earn the successful office, money and the finer things in life?

It is time to stop being flippant about your life. Be committed to life, your spouse, your career, your profession, and to excellence. That is what it means to have integrity. Many say they have the capacity, but so very few can prove it. Prove it to the world and prove it to yourself that you have the strength of character to endure the hardships. It is these hardships that make us grow and turn us into people of character.

Doctor's Goals, Visualizations, Limiting Beliefs, and Negative Self-talk

The Doctor
8. Doctor's Goals and Visualization

PYRAMID OF CHIROPRACTIC SUCCESS

"Where there is no vision, the people perish."
—Proverbs 29:18

There is a lot of power in stating where you want to go in life. Some people's process is ready, shoot, aim, rather than ready, aim, shoot which is the natural and logical method. Where is one supposed to shoot if they are not aiming? Sadly enough, many people are shooting for goals that they have no idea they have. It is similar to shooting an arrow straight up in the air at nothing. We have no idea where it will land. The outcome may be favorable, or the arrow may hit you in the head, killing you instantly. Our world seems to have gone into warp speed, and it is more common to see managers scream, "ready, shoot, aim." But, it doesn't take a genius to realize that it is not the natural order of things. Yes, it works sometimes, but I wouldn't count on it.

Zig Ziglar once told a story of a famous archer who could hit the bull's eye of a target from a hundred yards away, and then take another arrow and split the first one. This is an amazing feat, no doubt, but then, Zig promised his audience that he could teach everyone to shoot better than the famous archer in 20 minutes—provided he blindfolded the archer and spun him around a few times, so he would not know where he was shooting. It is obviously a silly story, but it proved his point well. How can anyone hit a target they cannot see? In other words, how can you hit a goal you do not have?

I'll give you another example from, "Alice in Wonderland." When Alice is lost and asks the Cheshire cat which direction she must turn, he replies, "That depends. Where do you want to go?" Alice states that she does not know. So the cat replies, "Then, take any road you like."

You must know where you are headed in your life and in your business to reach success. Otherwise, your goal is an abstraction, a concept. Not a real thing that is tangible and definable. Life cannot be an abstraction. If you are to succeed, you must keep your eye on where you are aiming.

Do you have goals for your life, for your office, for your family, for your financial future? Are they written down? A recent study at Virginia Tech University found that only one percent of the population has written their goals *and* review them at least weekly. Do you know who that one percent is?

Millionaires.

Where is your business now? Where do you want it to be? Do you want to grow your office to see 1,000 patients a month and leave it to your son, or do you want to sell it when you turn 60 years old? Define your dream outcome, and then start to devise steps that will help you get there. Growth is not accomplished in one giant step. It is generally gradual. Determine what must be done at each milestone of your growth, and what is needed to propel you to the next milestone. Should you hire an associate once you reach a patient load of 500 visits per month? Do you need to hire another front office staffer once you hit 600 patients per month?

You must devise a plan of action and see it to the end. It is common for a doctor to write goals and then not want to change. When a doctor does that, they are acting more like an employee rather than the business owner. Business owners treat their business like it is a strategic game. They know that in order to grow a business, things must change and be modified to support the new level of growth.

To excel, one must change. Employees hate to change and the doctor who acts like an employee especially hates change because the addition of more staff required means more money and more time managing people. These are two things that chiropractors hate to do. Don't chicken out on your strategic plan. Follow through and take your business to the next level.

I have heard many doctors say that they have goals, but not written down. I do salute them in accomplishing the first step. They are already doing better than 96 percent of the population, according to the Virginia Tech study. Writing down your thoughts brings them from the abstract to the real.

The mind is a powerful organ; in that I have no doubt. But its thoughts are not physical. They are mental and metaphysical. Writing down your goals brings the metaphysical to the physical. Now that your goals are written down on paper they are there for the whole world to see.

You can take the physical paper the goals are written on and carry them around with you. You can tape it to your bathroom mirror or the window of your car where you can see them often. You have made yourself more accountable to the outcome and much more likely to reach your desired destination.

Write goals about every aspect of your life. Read them often, and don't be afraid to change them often. Life is an evolving experience, and it is okay to want something today, and then, 10 years from now, decide that it is no longer a priority. As you grow, so will your desires and your priorities. It is common for youth to desire material things. But as many people mature, they switch more to family, harmonious friendships, security, peaceful living, and leaving a legacy. As I said earlier, people want only that which they do not have. We crave only what we believe is missing.

I know a few billionaires, and I will tell you that they have written down goals. Don't, for one minute, think that writing down goals is some hairy fairy tactic. It is real, powerful, and necessary.

I have a statement that I say, to myself, and to patients that I would love to repeat here; "If you want to be something, mimic the actions of people that are already where you want to be." If rich people have written down goals and you want to be rich, why would you not follow their lead? If you wanted to be a couch potato, would you not mimic what couch potatoes do? If you wanted to be strong and healthy, would you not also mimic healthy people's actions?

This can seem simplistic, and it is meant to, because becoming what you want to be in life is not really that difficult. Simply copy people who are living the way you want to.

The affluent in society generally are better educated. So get a good education. They generally have a better vocabulary. So study your language and develop a large vocabulary. Rich people are generally cautious of where they spend their money. So think twice before you buy another car you don't need.

As stated earlier, I once heard that rich people in America in general read 17 books per year, 15 of which are nonfiction. You should also mimic this activity, if you want to be rich. It is amazing to me how few people actually read. I ask many people if they read on a daily basis. Most of the people tell me they haven't read a book in years. This, I believe, is a shame.

If you don't read it is no different if you didn't know how to read. We often pity the illiterate. But what is the difference if you have the reading skill, but consciously decide not to use it. There is definitely truth to the saying, "Readers are leaders."

You may have noticed that I used the word "generally" in the past few paragraphs. I stated that the affluent generally read 17 books a year. The reason I say generally is because you will always find a person who will prove such data wrong. Henry Ford, for instance, was not an academically oriented individual and probably didn't read much, yet he was a millionaire many times over.

I also have had patients to quote that their grandfather died at 90 years old and drank a bottle of whiskey every day for 60 years. There will always be people who defy reality. They go against the norm and still succeed. No doubt, these people exist, but why mimic the abnormal?

I choose to copy people who can give me my best opportunity.

I will not recreate the wheel. All I have to do to reach where I want to be is follow in the footsteps of those I want to mimic. If my billionaire friend has written down goals, you can be sure that I do as well.

I like to take my goal list a little further. Late, celebrated surgeon and thinker Maxwell Maltz stated "that a mind cannot tell the difference between reality and one that is imagined vividly." For this reason, I created a vision board.

A vision board is nothing more than a collection of pictures representing all that I desire in life affixed where I regularly can see them. There are not only material depictions on this board, but also symbols that represent the way I want to live. I have a large peace sign in the middle, which reminds me that I want peace and mutual harmony in my life, and with all of my relationships.

We all have days that feel like things are not going as

planned. These days can lower your energy and make you feel fatigued, and that your efforts have been in vain. I, too, have these days, and when I do, I take my vision board into a quiet room and sit looking at the board and all that it represents to me.

I let my mind wander and I close my eyes, and see that beautiful cabin I desire on the mountain lake. I envision trout fishing on that lake with my son and the peace of mind that image brings.

I may picture my office full of patients and those patients referring others. I picture my associates finally getting what I have been trying to teach them. I imagine their life growing and expanding, thus creating a ripple effect of my influence.

Not long after I perform this visualization technique, my mood, and state of mind return to the value of my goals. This time apart from the frustration allows me to more than simply write down the goals; it allows me to feel the success of attaining my goals, even before I actually am there.

The mind responds to emotions much stronger than words. By feeding it the emotions I desire, I can better influence my outcome.

At this juncture, your logical mind may be starting to jump in and tell you that all this mental imagination and goal setting is fine for some people, but not for you. You are a logical person, and only other people can succeed—not you. You are only average, and therefore, you should expect an only average life, not a life filled with your wildest dreams. You figure you need some concrete actions—not this New Age crap.

This is what I call limited beliefs and negative self-talk.

I often picture an angel sitting on one of my shoulders and

the devil sitting on the other, like we used to see in cartoons. The angel keeps telling me that I can do anything I desire if I properly use my God-given talents. Meanwhile, the devil tells me that I am weak, average, untalented, and not worthy of attaining my heaven on earth. You know the message: "You can't be a millionaire. That happens only to special people—not you."

We all have these two sides to our psyche, and negative self-talk is to be expected. However, you cannot allow your mind to run too long down this path. You are special. You have been endowed with greatness. There is no one on earth quite like you. You have gifts that, if tapped, can produce all that you desire. God would not put desires in your mind and not give you the tools to attain them. That would be cruel.

We all have to deal with limited beliefs and negative self-talk. This is not a problem unique to you. I can assure you that if you are having problems in your financial realm, work, or relationships, you are a victim to some amount of limiting beliefs.

Presidents of the United States have limiting beliefs. I'm sure the president has wondered at some point how the world is going to be put back on track, and if he is truly the right one for the job. The billionaire who owns the software company is debating somewhere today if he can pull off a business deal he is working on. We all get down on ourselves sometimes. But the winner is the person who realizes what is happening. They have learned to give themselves a pep talk, and get their mind away from failure and back on track to success. If they kept the limited talk going, nothing would get done.

Have you ever fallen into this trap of a downward spiral of

negative self-talk? Let's say that your spouse is not where they are supposed to be at a certain time. An hour goes by, maybe two hours. Where does your mind start to drift? Are they having an affair? Were they in a car accident, and are they dead on the side of the road? Then, all of the sudden, they walk in the door and tell you why they were late. They forgot, or they were stuck in traffic. To you, the excuse just doesn't seem good enough.

Your mind will drift in a downward spiral. You begin to make up stories in your mind about what they could have been doing all this time, and how inconsiderate they were. You keep repeating these stories in your mind until they seem real, and then before you know it, you are in a big fight over some small thing. Later you realize that the argument was your fault because you really had an argument over nothing except what you conjured up in your mind.

This is what can happen when you let the devil on your left shoulder run for too long with wild – and dark and un-true—imaginings. It happens in relationships, at work, with friends, your business, your goals, insurance companies, or any other aspect of your life. Take control of your mind and stop this game before it destroys your business and your life.

We can create problems that don't exist, but yet we feel justified in our actions, when really it is our crazy minds running wild. Don't talk yourself into negativity and failure. We can do anything we desire as long as we don't mind working for it. But, our minds must stay focused and in line with our ultimate vision.

In general, chiropractors are artists at delivering spinal manipulations. They are not generally business people, and therefore they believe that the key to business success is to be highly skilled at their art. They believe that if they are struggling in their clinic, they have to get more training in clinical skills and chiropractic technique. Is this true or is it a limiting belief?

It is impossible to answer that question for everyone, but it has been my experience that more clinical skills will not make a chiropractor successful. However, belief is a choice. We live in a free country and we are free to think and believe anything we want.

It was expected that all business would decrease during the last recession we experienced in 2008, and for many people it did. Daily I would get junk email showing me how to recession-proof my office if I only went to this or that seminar. My office, on the other hand, grew 35% in 2008 and then another 20% in 2009. Does this fact shake up your reality? What is the real truth? When people told me there was a recession I said, "Maybe, but I choose not to participate." I programmed my mind not to expect this loss in business, and I didn't.

The way that you frame your questions in your mind may dramatically affect your negative self-talk. If you ask, "Why can't I get new patients?" your mind will tell you, "Because you are an idiot." If however, you ask the question, "How can I get new patients?" or "How can I get more new patients?" Then your mind will turn on and start giving you more productive answers.

It is only natural to question yourself from time to time. Without this ability, you would jump without first looking and that can get you into big trouble. You have to learn when to question your actions and when it is simply your negative side just trying to drag you down. Listen more to the angel on your right shoulder. That is the side of you that will bring you to the Promised Land.

The Doctor's Response to Failure

The Doctor
9. Doctor's Response to Failure

PYRAMID OF CHIROPRACTIC SUCCESS

"It is impossible for anyone to like to fail, but if you don't learn how to capitalize on your failures, you will never do as much as you could have done."
—Charlie "Tremendous" Jones

Nobody likes to fail, but we have all done it, and we will do it again. Failure is a part of life. I am less concerned with a person's failure as I am with how he responds to the failure.

I remember hearing the definition of a hero not as someone who doesn't experience fear, but as a person who does what is needed to be done regardless of their fear. That can also be the definition of courage.

It is important to treat failure with this courageous attitude. We will all do things that blow up in our face. We get married to the wrong person. Get in business with the wrong person. We try marketing techniques that backfire when promoting our practice. We get sued when we least expect it. These things happen, but what did you learn from these mistakes? That is where the growth lies. That is what separates the strong from the weak. A business hero is someone who does what has to be done regardless of fear. But the coward is a person who is paralyzed with fear and does nothing. They maintain the status quo.

Business is not for the weak-spirited. It is for the fighter. Failure is part of the game. The person who wins the game is the person who does the most—wins some and loses some, learns from the failures and becomes a better business leader. Never feel bad about your failures. If you realize that you created it, take responsibility, so then you are in a better position to learn and grow.

I have made more mistakes than I care to mention. Some mistakes have cost me a quarter of a million dollars. That stings, but it is these deeper cuts that forced me to learn. It was an expensive education, but one that I will never forget.

For example, if you have an upset patient who claims you or your staff did something wrong, get to the bottom of the story. Don't sweep it under the rug like a coward. Find out what went wrong and fix it.

There will always be an upset patient. Some patients can get gold service and expect platinum. I used to have sleepless nights over these complaints, but now I have a meeting with my staff about the problem, fix it, and sleep well at night.

I'm sure that you have done advertising at some point that has not been effective. Don't complain that you lost all your money. Consider it a learning experience, and vow never to repeat it.

If you practice with this mentality, you will soon determine that time will make you successful because, through a process of elimination and self-discovery, you will become better at the art of business. If you make enough mistakes, you will eventually win.

Sharpening Your Saw

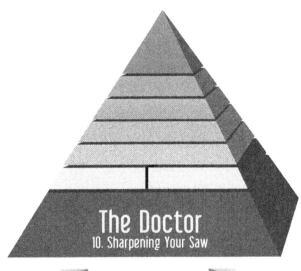

The Doctor
10. Sharpening Your Saw

PYRAMID OF CHIROPRACTIC SUCCESS

"I don't have time to sharpen the saw, the man said emphatically. I'm too busy sawing."

—Stephen Covey

This concept was taken from the book "Seven Habits of Highly Effective People" By Stephen Covey. I have, however, placed a chiropractic business slant on his approach.

I see this idea of "sharpening your saw" can be taken two

ways. First, one can say this statement means that you need to keep your skills sharp in business to allow you to be competitive in business. Second, it could mean that you have to keep yourself sharp through the process of rejuvenation and relaxation. I believe that sharpening your saw can mean both.

As a chiropractor, it is important to keep you skills fresh and expanding. Learn to become a better adjuster, a better clinician, better at documentation, and overall a better person. Your patients pay you to be the best, so continuously strive to be the best.

There are many venues that help us grow as a chiropractor: Palmer College of Chiropractic *Lyceum* Seminars, Parker seminars, nutrition seminars, state association gatherings and many, many more continuing education venues. Make sure that you are someone who has the joy to learn new things so you can give more to the world.

In my dealings with struggling chiropractors however, I rarely see this acquisition of knowledge being their limiting factor to business success. The other side of the coin is a whole different thing. The struggling doctor often feels that he or she must spend every minute in their office. They believe the key to getting more patients is to be in the office more, just in case someone walks in the door. They do this at their own expense, in that they are mentally and physically fatigued.

Earlier, I stated that in order for God to give you patients to manage and help, you must be in high spirits and at an energy level greater than the person you are trying to aid. If you are fatigued, the only people that will show up are the lowest energy people in the world. These are the people whom we all hate to treat. These are the people who make you feel drained every time they enter you door. You must take care of yourself first, and then you will be able to take care of patients.

I used to be the doctor who believed that the more I worked, the better off I would be financially. The statement is logical and I am a logical person. However, in the fall of 2003 I found myself tired and irritable with everything. For that reason, my business was starting to slide backwards. In 2004, I took 10 major vacations. I was not out of the office much. I simply took one extra-long weekend each month. My wife and I would go to Mexico, on a cruise, or rent a cabin in Gatlinburg. It was one of the best years that I can remember. At the end of 2004, I was going over my yearly statistics and discovered that I had seen more patients and collected more money than any previous year by at least 25%.

The thought was so counterintuitive that I didn't know what to make of it. How is it that I could have worked less and made more money? Because, whenever I was working at the office, I was much more engaged, I was on task, I was more emotionally sound, and I was no longer mentally fatigued. I was on purpose. I was learning the art of balance. I learned that if I balance my life of service to humanity with rest and relaxation, I prosper. I learned that I couldn't neglect myself for others. So, I can assist others more when I take care of my own needs.

This is a major lesson that young doctors have not yet mastered. It is counterintuitive, and for that reason, they have to fight the mentality that they have to be at the office at all times to be successful.

By the same token, I have had a few doctors who worked for me who thought it was okay to hardly ever be at the office.

Their personal goals were about only lifestyle, free time and not about financial gain. They took my teachings way too far. This practice reeks of lack of commitment and I am happy to say those doctors no longer work for me. Any general rule can be taken too far. I do have to be physically present sometime if I expect business success.

You must also do something daily to keep your mind focused and relaxed. Many will exercise daily, have a hobby, or spend time with friends to rejuvenate their soul. I personally get up in the morning an hour before everyone else and read with a good cup of coffee. That is my form of peaceful time that is mine. It is my time for me and only me.

Burnout is a very common problem in our profession. You need time to recharge your soul. Patients need you to be 100%. They are relying on you to stay energetic, focused and on purpose. To accomplish that, you must first take care of yourself. I used to have the problem of feeling that if I left work, the office would fall apart. I have later learned that is egotistical garbage. The world can exist without me for a few days, especially if I come back better than before I left.

PART II

Introduction

The next section of this book is more for the left-brain domi-
nant person. The first half of this book dealt more with the
personality characteristics and mental state of the doctor, the
second section deals more with the concrete aspects that
come with growing a business.

The topics covered in the remainder of this book were not
covered very well in your school curriculum and represent
one of the key reasons why chiropractors struggle in private
practice. Some students are naturally business minded, but,
from my experience, they are rare. I'm sure that even the
more seasoned business doctor could also learn something
new from part two of this book.

The top 25% of figure 1 represents the academic topics
of **The Pyramid of Chiropractic Success**. Each chapter will
be designated to cover one of these important areas to thor-
oughly explain their significance.

These topics will sometimes make people uncomfort-
able. People question their math skill and are easily confused

with the interpretations of business statistics. I will attempt to keep the math to a minimum and completely describe what can be inferred from each stat. There is no point in plugging in numbers if the outcome means nothing to you or has no value. Numbers are a businessperson's lifeline. Numbers let you know if your business is on the right track or if it is failing. When the numbers are calculated, often one can see problems and fix them before it is too late.

Top businessman, entrepreneur and investment expert Keith Cunningham states that "business is an intellectual sport," and earlier you heard me say, "Success is a mental sport." I have attended Cunningham's classes on business management, and I can tell you he is one of the sharpest business people I know. So, yes, business is an intellectual sport, but, like all sports, if you want to play, you have to first learn the rules and the terminology necessary to communicate to other business leaders.

To learn more about Cunningham and possibly attend one of his classes, you can find him at www.keystothevault.com.

I have mentioned several times that you don't have to follow me in order to be successful. You don't have to control your thoughts, your behavior, you don't have to be a leader and you don't have to learn the terminology of business to be successful. However, if you don't, the cards are stacked against you.

Why try and recreate the wheel? Learn the concepts throughout this book and you are much more likely to reach your goals.

As I begin part II of this book I want to inform you again that of all the people I have helped through the years, 75%

of their difficulty is not what I am about to show you. It has been what we already covered in part 1. **The Pyramid of Chiropractic Success** is heavily weighted to limitations I see in the doctors' personality, not their inability to determine statistics. But like all things, the whole is connected through a complex web of interactions. For instance, if a chiropractor has a bad attitude and refuses to listen to others, it is unlikely he or she will crunch the statistics and other numbers necessary to business success. People who are unable to see themselves as the problem will not look at their financial elements to determine where they are lacking. They are more likely to blame outside forces.

3

Patients and Business Practices

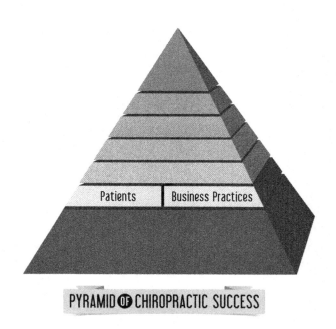

PYRAMID **OF** CHIROPRACTIC SUCCESS

"Business is an intellectual sport."

—Keith Cunningham

In my first draft of **The Pyramid of Chiropractic Success**, I first placed business practices as being more important than patients. I have since modified that original pyramid, because

I have met chiropractors who have very little business sense, but are still running what appear to be successful practices.

They compensate for their lack of business savvy by being very good at all other areas of the pyramid. They have a large influx of new patients because they are great, friendly people. They know how to communicate with the patient for patient education. They know how to get referrals. They have a great attitude about life and they are great doctors and leaders.

When I talk to them about their business practices, I quickly see their ignorance about classical business statistics and financials. They may be able to carry on in practice for years and never have a problem with business regression, but that is very unlikely. It is likely they will experience difficulties at some point in the future, and since they have no idea how to monitor their practices, they will not see the early warning signs that they are dying. Even if they do see the early warning signs, they will have no idea how to fix their growing problem. The truth is in the numbers. They do not lie. They cannot lie.

The money collected in an office goes first to pay all of your expenses, and your wage is determined on what is left over. Bad business practices are like having a leaky bucket—one that is leaking money every day. You can still have money after your expenses are paid as long as you have a steady inflow of new patients. But if the patient volume drops, you have a bucket that will eventually run dry. Improve your business knowledge and plug the hole so you can take more income for yourself.

Nevertheless, if you can somehow get a large volume of patients through your office and maintain the flow, you do not need to know the art of business management. This is risky business of course—one that I don't recommend and I believe is a ticking time bomb.

Patients are the key ingredients to a successful office. You cannot bill insurance without seeing patients, and your landlord will not accept chickens as payment for rent. There are generally two ways to practice in the chiropractic world. You can have a high volume practice where you bill little and make the difference up in volume. Or you can have a lower volume practice where you spend more time with the patient and bill more services.

Straight chiropractors and high volume practice will do little to no rehabilitation, passive modalities, supportive taping and X-rays. They may see five hundred patients a week and bill $40 each. They may have very little staff assistance, and generally, they are constantly doing large campaigns to try and get new patients in the door.

I used to work in an office like that in South America and swore that when I came back to the United States, I would never practice that way again. I see nothing wrong with that type of practice, but it takes a very special type of personality to run an office like that, one that borders on ADHD.

I would come home in the evening exhausted and wishing I hadn't gone to chiropractic school. I was heading for burnout, and I knew it was a practice that I could not maintain.

Today, I practice a much slower pace, one where I spend time with the patient. I adjust them, do my own stretching, muscle rehabilitation, passive modalities, and kenesio taping. I keep my billing high and my volume low. This is more along the line of my personality. I make the same, if not more, than the high-volume chiropractor, and I have less chance of burnout.

The choice on how you practice is completely up to you, and I have little judgment either way. Choose a style that fits your personality, desires, goals, and family values.

If, however, you choose to go my direction in lower volume and better billing, it will be important to know more about business practices and statistics.

Every business owner should have a CPA to do payroll, taxes and financial strategizing. Most people get a cash flow statement, balance sheet and asset/liability report from their CPA if not quarterly at least annually. Most doctors I know take this report and tuck it in a folder thinking it is for tax purposes only. That is not the case. There are loads of information on that sheet that lets you know where you were last year as compared to this year and where all of your expenses are going. You can graph this information each year to keep an eye on your outstanding bills, rising cost of expenses, and to see if you have too many staff and many other invaluable information.

It is absolutely impossible for me to go over the information you can get from these CPA reports in this book. That information is so vast you would need a separate book on the topic. I do suggest that you sit with your CPA at the end of each year and get their opinion as to the growth or death of your business. If you would like to do this on your own, you can visit www.keystothevault.com and download a computer program that fully explains the importance of financial statements. This program was created by Keith Cunningham and his company, Keys to the Vault. It has been a pleasure getting to know Keith. He is a financial wizard and his service to humanity in the form of financial education is greatly appreciated.

In general, you need to realize that your assets, both

your physical assets and intellectual assets, are used to create sales. Sales minus your expenses result in profits, but you can't spend profits. Profits minus retained earnings and taxes will produce spendable cash. It is this spendable cash that can buy things such as more assets. Refer to figure 6 as a representation of the above statement.

Figure 6.
Financial Statement

Many businesses have gone bankrupt because they believed that the key to survival is to produce more sales. That can be a way to increase cash, but you can't spend sales, and it is not the only way. In general, when you increase sales, your expenses also increase. There comes a time when the increase in sales does not produce the returns in cash. It is important, as the business leader, to determine that cutoff amount. To push sales higher and higher may not necessarily increase your cash and thus your wage. Poorly run offices may have lots of sales but no cash.

For example, you may give incentives to your staff to get more sales (patients). You get the patients and pay the staff their bonus, but these patients end up not paying their bill. You are left spending more money than was gained.

It stands to reason that the more money you spend on marketing, the more patients you get in your office. If however, you spend too much money in a TV advertisement, or billboard, to get these patients you may also lose you money in the long run.

Sales are not the only way to get more money. You could cut your expenses, decrease your tax load, pay off a loan, stop buying assets or retain less earning. All of these methods would increase your income. You have to determine when it is best to do each method in order to maximize your return.

Jay Abraham, another financial and business genius, states that there are really only three ways to grow a business.

1) Increase the number of sales
2) Increase the amount of money for each transaction
3) Increase the frequency of repurchase

To make this principle chiropractic, we can say that the only way to grow your office is to see more patients, increase the amount each patient or their insurance will pay you, and lastly, increase the number of times you supply treatment.

Obviously, one has to bring ethics into this equation when you are talking about health care. It would be unethical for you to treat a patient who doesn't need treatment. In the insurance world, to convince a person they need treatment when in fact they do not is called baiting. Baiting is a serious accusation in the insurance world. You can lose your provider relationship with the insurance company or worse, your chiropractic licenses if you are found guilty of such practices.

Offering free care, and even discounted care has to be handled within the confines of your state board of examiners. I would suggest that you get all marketing material approved by your board before releasing it into the general public.

It is also unethical and morally unsound to bill for services that were not rendered in your office or for services not needed to assist the patient. This is also a serious insurance breach of contract and can also result in losing your relationship with the insurance company, or have to repay all the money they paid you, not to mention the ill will created by the patient who believes that you cheated them. This is neither legal nor sound business.

Lastly, we have to talk about the ethical issue of overtreating a patient. I know that in chiropractic school, we feel that it is impossible to overtreat a patient. The more chiropractic manipulations the patient receives, the better. Insurance carriers no longer pay for maintenance care or wellness care. They pay for acute care only. Make sure that if you convince a patient that they need to be on wellness care, which I believe is a good idea, that they are fully aware that this type of care will not be covered by their insurance. Insurances will ask for their money back if they feel you have billed for treatment that would be considered maintenance.

In business, there is something worse than not getting paid for your services rendered, and that is paying back the money once you have already spent it on expenses and taxes. This is something that all practitioners dread and should be prevented at all cost.

So how is it you can follow Jay Abraham's advice and still stay within the confines of your ethics? First of all, there is nothing wrong with seeing more volume. You can always grow by seeing more people as long as those people need your help. And let's face it, who doesn't need a chiropractic adjustment from time to time?

You can increase the dollar amount of your transaction by supplying more service to the patient. If the patient is inflamed, it is legitimate to put EMS on the point of injury. If the patient has muscular problems, and most do, it is fine to stretch the affected area or do trigger point work. You can offer a massage done by a staff member. You can sell vitamins, or cervical pillows. There are countless, legitimate ways to increase the point of sale amount to increase your business.

Chiropractic is based on the foundation of wellness care. We can increase the frequency of repurchase by properly educating patients, thus increasing the amount of individuals that transition to a wellness lifestyle. Just remember, insurance does not pay for this treatment.

The following are a few examples of the proper application of Jay Abraham's process. I have placed numbers to this concept so you can better see the application and how small changes can make big improvements to your bottom line when they are implemented in tandem.

Table #1

Initial Office Statistics - Table 1

#Customers/month	Average Sale ($)	Frequency	Total Monthly Income ($)	Total Yearly Income ($)
100 individual customers per month	$50	6 visits	$30,000	$360,000

Table # 1 illustrates your office before the application of Jay Abraham's principles. Of all the doctors whom I have talked to over the years, many feel that it is a very easy task to increase these numbers by 10%. This means a 10% increase in the number of customers, average sale and frequency of visit.

In Table #2, I will show you the compounding effect of this increase. The number of customers will be increased to 110, the average sale will be increased to $55/visit, and I will increase the average frequency of visits to 6.6 visits per month. Before I show you the effect of this compounding, I would like to first tell you that this increase is extremely easy to do. And it has been my experience that I can increase average sale amounts by 20 to 50%. This increase, of course, would make this illustration even more powerful.

Table #2

10% in Office Statistics - Table 2

#Customers/month	Average Sale ($)	Frequency	Total Monthly Income ($)	Total Yearly Income ($)
110 individual customers per month	$55	6.6 visits	$39,930	$480,000

As you can plainly see, that modification resulted in a 33% office growth in income. The best thing about this amount of growth is that it was so subtle that it rarely increases office expenses. Therefore, the extra $120,000 per year ends up being income for the doctor. How would you like to make and additional $120,000 per year?

Small changes can make a big difference. This is only one of the many exercises that I perform with clients to show them the ease and power of expanding their business.

The remainder of this chapter will be designated to office statistics. Before your heart starts to flutter with the memories and nightmares of that college statistics course you took, I will tell you that these statistics that I offer for consideration are not only easy, but are also the window into the function of your office.

It is my hope that you see the value of business statistics by the end of this chapter. You must also be able to properly interpret and infer what each number is really telling you.

The following is a list of the general statistics that I do monthly in each of my offices. There are many more numbers that I can calculate, as compared to the list below, but I do not do them on a monthly bases. I do them, however, anytime I determine that something is going wrong with my general statistics.

Number of patients seen per month
Number of new patients seen per month
Number of patients seen per insurance carrier
Number of cash patients seen
Amount billed per insurance carrier per month
Amount collected per insurance carrier per month
Number of 98940, 98941, and number of 98942
Number of extremity adjustments per month
Number of EMS billed per month
Number of mechanical traction billed per month
Average number of codes per visit billed per month
Number of active care modalities billed per month
Number of X-rays taken per month
Number of established patient physicals performed per month
Number of joint taping per month
Patient visit average per doctor per month

I have an Excel spreadsheet constructed that does most of my statistic calculations for me. I simply plug in these values from the office software, print it out, and I get the values I am interested in.

I will now illustrate the calculations that I preform with the above values.

1) Amount billed per month/Number of patients seen = Average amount billed

You cannot collect money from an insurance company unless it is billed. I am not an advocate of billing for services not rendered. However, it has been my experience that doctors don't bill, or don't bill enough, for services rendered. You must know what it is that you can bill for as compared to insurance codes that are bundled together with other codes. At times, this may vary with individual insurance carriers. For instance, Medicare states that the exam is bundled together with the adjustment code, and therefore, you can't bill for both.

2) Amount Collected/Number of patients seen = Average income per visit

This statistic is extremely valuable but, it must be performed on an insurance-by-insurance basis. The amount insurance pays for a particular code varies dramatically. Therefore, to get the most from this statistic, you have to separate insurance carriers.

This statistic can show you which insurances pay the best. If the number is lower in a particular month, you know there is a billing issue because collections are delayed. This, along with the amount billed graphed over months, can let you know if you are slipping in your billing quality.

3) Average amount billed/Average income per visit = Collection ratio

It is a must to determine your collection ration for each insurance company. When a collection ratio is too high, it generally means that the insurance carrier is paying you quickly, or has a very high reimbursement rate. Collection ratios that are too low means you are either billing for services that are not covered by a particular insurance company, collections are being delayed due to requests for additional information, or that company simply pays very low as compared to other companies.

4) PVA (patient visit average) can be calculated monthly or yearly by determining how many visits each patient was in your office in a year/how many patients were seen.

Doctors with a low PVA show me that they are not educating their patients well enough, and therefore patients are not converting to wellness plans. It could also mean that the doctor is shy or has poor communication skill, and therefore does not instill confidence in the patient.

This area is the most difficult area to correct. It requires changing a person's personality and self-confidence. These are character flaws that are rooted at the core of an individual. But, like all things, it can be taught if the recipient really wants to learn. Refer to the first half of this book for an in-depth explanation and possible remedy for this condition.

5) Number of established exams/Number of patients seen = % of exams performed

It started back in school that chiropractors learned to hate doing exams. "All I want to do is adjust people," many would say. I hear that so many times I wouldn't even care to count.

When people hate to do something, they try as hard as possible to avoid doing it.

If the percentages of exams are too low, and they usually are, I know a doctor is inflicted with this hatred. Exams and diagnosis code changes are what tell an insurance company things are progressing, changing, or the patient has a new problem. It tells them that you know what you are doing. It is also one of the highest-paid codes through insurance companies, so it would behoove you to start doing more of them.

It is the right thing to do. It is what gets you paid, it is what will keep your business profitable. So stop complaining and do them.

6) Number of 98940/Number of patients seen = % of 98940

Do this also for the 98941 and 98942 as well. There is a percentage of each that is expected in the eyes of the insurance company, and if you are out of the norm seen across the country, you have a potential red flag. To be red-flagged by an insurance company means that you will be asked for additional information to process the claim. This can also be called a soft audit.

This not only slows down the process that gets you paid, it also opens up an opportunity for a hard audit. That is where the insurance company requests all of your files or shows up in your office to look at your files. Once they are finished, they tell you the percentage of errors they found and request that percentage of money back that they paid you over a certain amount of time.

Audits are not fun. They can cost you hundreds of thousands of dollars and you may even go bankrupt.

Doctors who are afraid of this audit will justify billing only the 98940. They believe that billing the lowest code will keep them under the radar. That is not true. Billing the same code is very abnormal and it does not keep you under the radar. It causes you to stick out, which is not a good thing. Repetitive and carbon copy billing is a no-no because it tells the insurance company that you are not really thinking about your treatment. Your procedure is to do the same on every patient you have, rather than individualize your treatment.

In addition to limiting the chance of an audit, you are losing a lot of money. It stands to reason that the 98941 is paid more than the 98940 and the 98942 is paid more than the 98941. Don't shortchange yourself because you are afraid of an audit. Practice correctly and you will get the most money with the least chance of an audit.

7) Number of extremity codes billed/Number of patients seen = % of extremities

I do this statistic for all the remaining codes. I do it for EMS, mechanical traction, active care procedures, kenesio taping, and X-rays. Determining the percentage of each of these codes allows the doctor to determine when they are dropping the ball and areas on which the doctor places too much emphasis.

If you do EMS on everyone, you are asking for trouble. EMS is for acute care only, and doing it on everyone tells the insurance company you run a cookie-cutter practice, and that is yet another red flag.

Some of these codes are the highest-paid services that we can perform in our office, and not billing them frequently enough can result in a struggling office. It has been my observation that doctors don't do a procedure not because they don't know how it is used, but because they get stuck in a rut of looking at a patient the same way on each visit. I have heard doctors say that their patients don't have many extremity complaints, but I know that is not true. If you listen to the patient, you will soon find out that most of them have a knee, shoulder, elbow or foot pain.

You are the best person to address this problem. You have a great knowledge of biomechanics, and you don't prescribe medication to mask the problem. The patient is asking for help. Step up and be the doctor you were meant to be.

8) Add up all the codes done/Number of patients seen = Average code/visit

This calculation is my bread and butter. This statistic allows me to know instantly if a doctor is collecting the highest amount per each patient encounter. If this number is too high, it is a guaranteed audit.

You have to learn to play in the gray area where you get the best income, but stay away from the spotlight.

This calculation will tell me instantly the skill of the doctor. I will know instantly if they know how to do passive care, active care, joint taping, home exercise training, or if they are a rack-'em-stack-'em doctor. Average codes per visit is one of the best numbers to determine and the most informative.

I have dealt with many doctors and thousands of patient

visits, and over the years, I have a good idea what the expected numbers for each statistic should be. I would never print them in this book or any other book. It opens up way too much liability for me. All I need is a doctor to follow my recommendations on what an acceptable number of codes per visit should be, get audited, lose and come after me because I printed it. He or she would claim that they was just following my recommendations. Sure, that wouldn't stand up in court but do I want that hassle? I think not!

Statistics are the window to any business. It is how you determine where you are, where you are going and possible methods on how to change your outcome. The office that does not perform business statistics is a ticking time bomb. It will either be ravished by the insurance companies or bankrupt.

Your office is your own back yard. Keep it clean.

4
Marketing

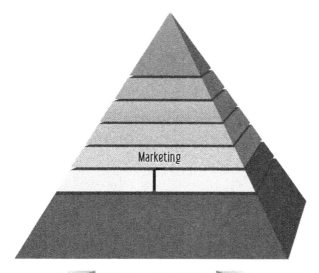

PYRAMID OF CHIROPRACTIC SUCCESS

*"The purpose of business is to produce customers…..
Marketing and innovation produce results; all the rest
are cost."*

—Peter Drucker

The topic of marketing can be very complex. With the advent
of the Internet, standard forms of advertising such as through
newspapers, direct mailing, radio and television have become

less and less effective. One has to be concerned about spending more money on the advertising campaign, as compared to the amount that is being earned from your effort. If it is not cost effective, what is the point of doing it?

Everyone in your town will try to sell you advertisement space on just about anything they can print a name on. I have been contacted by the chamber to place ads in their bulletins, and the local supermarket to place adds on shopping carts. The radio wants me to sponsor the local football team. You name it and people will hound you to spend your money. They claim that it will be effective because 50,000 shoppers will see your promotions while shopping. But really—who is looking for a chiropractor while they are picking up groceries?

I have tried just about every advertising method there is, not because I thought that it would work, but because I have been talked into advertising by a great sales pitch and the promise of results. I can tell you from experience that rarely do any of these methods work. When they do seem to get a few new patients, they are not quality patients who are looking to get well and become lifelong wellness patients. For the most part, advertising is a frustrating, money losing game.

Is it all a waste? Of course not. But be aware that marketing without you personally sacrificing your time and energy is not lucrative.

Marketing can be separated into two major categories: internal marketing and external marketing. External marketing is done outside of your office in an attempt to connect to potential clients. When we think about external marketing, we generally talk about yellow page advertisements, newspaper, or radio spots. But this can also include spinal screening, or health fairs at local factories.

External marketing is expensive, and generally has low returns on your investment. The exception to that statement is with spinal screenings and health screenings. These methods can be very effective if they are done properly, but if not done correctly, you can lose a full day in the office with no gain from your efforts.

No one likes to do spinal screenings. They can be degrading, frustrating and make you feel like a second-class citizen rather than an upstanding doctor. I have to admit, though, I have done them and I have gotten a lot of patients that way. However, when I became popular and busy in my town, it was the first activity I dropped.

Internal marketing are methods of advertising in your office. It includes what educational material that you provide for your patients, slide shows in your waiting room, and most importantly, how you communicate with your patients. If you properly educate your patients they will refer other people. If you neglect to educate your patients, they will get well, not return, not convert to wellness care, and not refer.

Your best form of advertising is, and always will be, word of mouth. It is free, effective, and you get a much better, quality patient. Your good patients that think you are God's gift to the world will refer you other great patients who also think you are awesome. To master the art of business success, you have to master the art of getting referrals. Do that, and you will never have to pay for marketing again.

Daily, I get spam email in my junk folder that tells me some new way to market myself on the internet. I look at those emails and chuckle, "Who wants more patients? Not me." I don't want more patients. I want good patients. Patients who want to get well, patients who will follow up on my recommendations, patients who will refer others.

Mass marketing does not promise that. They just promise more bodies. When I was a struggling, new chiropractor, I wanted more people, but now that I am more seasoned, I realize that method of attracting patients is a revolving door. When you don't spend time educating the patient who is already in your office, you will be forced to keep doing external marketing to get more noncompliant patients.

Figure 7 illustrates the proper relationship between internal and external marketing. Initially in your practice, external marketing is a must. Nobody in town knows who you are, and it is your responsibility to change that perception. You have to get your name out via external means. As your patient volume increases, you should lean towards internal marketing where you are properly educating your patients and increasing referrals as your patient volume increases. Once you are doing well with the referrals and internal marketing, there will be no need to continue to do external marketing, which at that point you can discontinue.

Figure 7.

INTERNAL vs EXTERNAL MARKETING

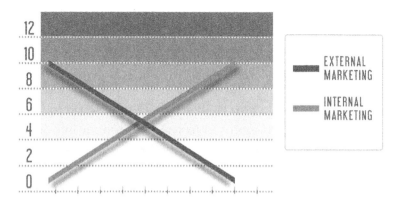

The key to having a long-term, successful, lucrative practice is to reach the point where external marketing is not needed as quickly as possible. Chiropractors who don't need to advertise after their first year in practice are guaranteed success. Those doctors who continue external means of attracting patients after years of practice have a difficult time retaining patients and operate minimally on referrals. This doctor is destined to struggle forever. The cost of attracting patients will eventually rise too high, and his profit margins will decrease as the years pass, resulting in a poor business model.

How do you get more referrals? How do you keep the patient in your office for wellness? You love the patient you already have.

Some chiropractors want to treat hundreds of patients a day, and get to know no one. There are a few people out there who can maintain that lifestyle, but that personality is extremely rare, and I am not one of them. These people, when you meet them, act as if they don't have time to talk to you because their mind is moving so fast they can't concentrate on one thing. It is similar to ADHD, and I find it very distracting. There is nothing wrong with practicing this way if that is who you are, but few can keep up the pace needed to practice this way over the long term.

I have learned that you have to give the patient more than they expect and be a part of their family to hold on to them. Sadly, many patients are used to waiting an hour in doctors' waiting rooms, and then being rushed when they eventually get to see the doctor. You have to show them that they are important and that their time is valuable. You have to be on time. Talk to them about their hopes and dreams, as well as their problems at work and home.

If you become a part of their family, you cannot be easily replaced. They will never leave you for the doctor across the street who offers care $5 cheaper than you. They will refer their friends to you and then you can become a part of their family as well. Before you know it, you will be treating just about everyone in town and you will have branded yourself. You will be the indispensable chiropractor.

Practicing that way, I can still see 120 to 150 patients a week. That gives me a great wage, and when I became too busy, rather than seeing more patients, I hired an associate doctor to grow with me. This formula is not difficult and it is much more rewarding, at least for me.

I send my patients a gift certificate for Christmas to use in my office. I send them thank you letters for referring patients to me. I call them when I am concerned about something happening in their life. I give them my opinion on vitamins, exercises, medication, and financial concerns they may have. I have patients cry on my shoulder when a loved one passes away and I have them celebrate with me when they get a job promotion. I am genuine and I care about their life.

Besides, business is not about you or your product. It is about the client. Don't fall in love with your service. That is only the means to the end. Love your patients and be dedicated to them. Make them feel special, intelligent, understood, and loved.

Initially, patients never want to open up to me. They are in my office because they have pain, and they want me to fix it. I use this opportunity to gain rapport. I will give you an example of how I gain rapport with the patient on the initial encounter.

"Mr. Jones, I have looked at your X-rays and completed your exam, and you will be happy to know that I found your problem." (At this point the patient is sitting, so sit next to them. Never try to gain rapport while standing higher than the patient. They will feel intimidated and will not really be listening to you.)

"You have a massive twist in your pelvis, and that is causing you to put all of your weight on your right leg. That is why your lower back hurts on the left, but your knee hurts on the right. I have no idea how this happened, but you are in the right place, because I fix this type of thing every day. Because you have had this pain more than a month, it will take me about a month to get rid of it, but you will probably feel 50% better in two weeks. However, when you feel somewhat better, I still need you to come in and get it completely fixed, or your pain will just come back. I know you work hard and are a busy guy, so you can't afford to be off work with back pain. So I will work as quickly as I can. If you don't get this fixed, you will eventually ruin your right knee."

In the above dialogue, I first got on the patient's level, a simple action that told him he and I are equals. That will make him feel special and instantly gain rapport. I then told him what was wrong, in words he could understand, which validated his pain. I told him he was in the right place and that I fix this type of problem often. That gave him hope and assurance I know what I am doing.

Then, I gave him a time line on improvement and what to expect as he improved. I took all the guesswork out of his concerns, and he is happy he came to me. Never milk a patient for a referral on the first few visits. It won't work, and you will look like a peddler.

There is, however, a great time to plug a patient for referrals, and it is more effective than all other times. And that is the golden visit. The golden visit has been described as the visit when your patient enters into your office with a gleam in their eye and a bounce in their step. They are finally feeling much better and they tell you that they owe it all to you. That is the day that they think you hung the moon.

If you have been in practice more than a few months, you know exactly what I am talking about. The golden visit is so obvious to the doctor that the patient might as well have a sign around his or her neck reading, "GOLDEN VISIT."

The golden visit is not at any particular treatment date.

It can be the third visit or the tenth visit, which is difficult to predict, since all patients heal at different rates. Nonetheless, on the golden visit, that is when you plug your patients for referrals. People with a poverty mentality will oftentimes think this practice as being shady. But I do not find it despicable to ask your patients if they know if there is someone else you can help.

Good patients want you be successful, and will go to great lengths to aid you in your growth. There is, however, a good way to ask for referrals, and as usual, there is a way to come off looking shady. Do it correctly and you will grow your office very rapidly. Do it wrong and you will be the office that people avoid.

The following is an example of how I would handle the golden visit. Keep in mind I do not use scripts, and for that reason, the exact words would vary each time and with each patient. I want my words to sound genuine and individualized, which is exactly how I feel, so the tone of caring always come through.

> Mary: *Doc, I don't know what you did last visit, but I am feeling so much better. I can touch my toes again and I can really start to see light at the end of the tunnel.*

> Doctor: *Mary that is good news. Go ahead and get on the table and let me look at your spine so I can really see how you are doing.*

> I continue to do my regular check-up.

Doctor: *Mary, your spine is looking so much better. No wonder you are feeling better. I saw a few things wrong, but not half as many compared to your last visit.*

Mary: *Yes, Doc. I feel so much better, thanks to you.*

Doctor: *Come up and sit on the table. I want to talk to you about something. Mary, you are now beginning to see what I can do to help people. Chiropractic is amazing and it is one of my goals to spread what we do all over the world. Can you only imagine how many people are hurting out there and simply taking pain meds to cover it up?*

I'm so glad you were smart enough to get in here so I could help you. But I need your help and the help of all my patients to help me spread what you now know. I'm sure that you have friends, family, or just acquaintances that could use my help. Please, for the love of God, send them in here. I rely on my best patients referring people to me and I would love to put you in that category. So could you help me do that? Do you know someone we could help?

Mary: *Sure, Doc. I know lots of people who need you. I'm already trying to get my mom to come and see you.*

Doctor: *Excellent, Mary. A referral is the most sincere form of flattery. When one patient refers another, we know you appreciate what we are doing here.*

This type of dialogue is very effective. It deepened my

rapport with Mary, it told her that I have goals of healing the world, and it made her a part of that very large, altruistic purpose. People want to be a part of something larger than themselves, and if you hit the right nerve on a patient, they will refer you loads of patients.

After this conversation, place a star or some other indicating feature in her chart to remind you to ask her again next visit if she at least tried to send someone to you. Believe me, they will. The star is also to warn you not to milk a patient for referrals every visit. If you continue with this line of conversation each visit, you will look desperate and you will not get a referral and you will probably lose the patient you already have.

Another form of internal marketing is to get your best patients to give you a testimonial. Create a standardized sheet to make it easy for a patient to fill in and be sure to have a check box in the bottom that asks if you can use this testimonial for marketing purposes.

In my front lobby, a television plays informative health information and patient testimonials. I have also had patients talk on the radio on my behalf about how I changed their life for the better. Words coming directly from patients' lips are a hundred times more effective than your own words.

Even if the patient states that he or she does not want their testimonial used for marketing, you can still put it in a folder and call it your legacy folder. All people, especially chiropractors, have bad days and get down on themselves. What could be better than reading all of your success on days that you feel that you are wasting your time? It is guaranteed to pick you up and get you back on cloud nine.

Another form of internal marketing is to work your past customer list. Your computer can list all of the patients that have not been in for more than six months. Pull their chart and determine what they were in for and see if they finished their treatment plan, or did they fall off the wagon for some unknown reason. Get your staff to call them and tell them that the doctor was going over old charts and noticed that they never followed through on their treatment plan. You are trying to sound casual and concerned and you are just checking in to see that things are going okay and that maybe they should come in for a checkup.

It is amazing how many people will come back in once you call, or shortly afterward. The key is to put you on the front part of their brain. Over the past six months, they have forgotten about you and have learned to live with their aches and pains. Now, you have brought it to their awareness, and all they can think about is coming to see you.

There are many other forms of internal marketing, but I have decided to finish this chapter about the best form of marketing that will ensure you success over the long term. And that is transitioning patients to wellness care. At some point in the future of your career, I hope that you will never need another new patient because you are so swamped with wellness patients that you have no time to treat or market to new clients.

Like all other communication in your office, there is a good time to talk about wellness care to patients to have optimal effectiveness. I spread my conversation over at least 2 or 3 visits. When a patient is nearing the end of acute care treatment, you can sense uneasiness in his or her tone. They are thinking that there is no need to continue, since they are feeling much better. You have to learn to detect this timing and implant another thought in their head, or they will not return for their last treatment.

Near the end of acute care, I will say, *"Well, Jim, you are looking so much better and we are almost finished with your care. I do, however, want to warn you that this is when most people don't show up for their last few appointments, and within a few weeks or months they are back in here with the same problem. I hope you are smarter than that."*

I hope by now you have noticed a trend that everyone wants to be considered smart, and when you implant that seed into their minds, they are much more likely to follow through with your recommendations.

On the next to last visit I will say something along the lines of the following:

Doctor: *Jim I'm going to schedule you one month down the road. You have only one more visit left, and if you look and feel good after one month, we can be done. But, Jim, I want to let you know that you do have a second option. Remember when you first came in here how bad you felt? You couldn't sleep, you couldn't work and you just felt horrible.*

Jim: *Yes, I do, Doc. How could I forget?*

Doctor: *Why would you ever want to go back to that? Since we have done so much work with your spine, it is looking so much better. We have gained so much ground.*

Why would you want to lose what we have already ac-complished? If you wait to feel bad before you come back, we are going to have to do this process all over again. Why don't you think about coming in here on a maintenance schedule, and feel this good forever?

Jim: *Well, I didn't know that was an option.*

Doctor: *Sure, Jim, that is an option. I have hundreds of patients who get in here once a month for a check-up. It is so much easier keeping people well compared to getting them well. You don't have to make a commitment today, because I am going to see you in one month, anyway. Please think about it over this next month. I'm not your fa-ther, and you don't have to listen to me. And if you decide against maintenance care, that is fine. We will always be here to help you when the pain comes back, but I hope you sign up for a lifetime of prevention. Life is too short to be in pain.*

Jim: *Thanks Doc. I'll think about it.*

I'm not going to lie to you. Not everyone signs up for once-a-month preventative care, but a lot do. You will not be able to convince everyone, nor do you want to. The people who decide to do it will become close to you, and you will have a practice of friends. Those who decide against prevention still leave your office feeling free to come back. You planted the seed that even if you don't see them for two years, they know they will be welcomed back.

5
Staff

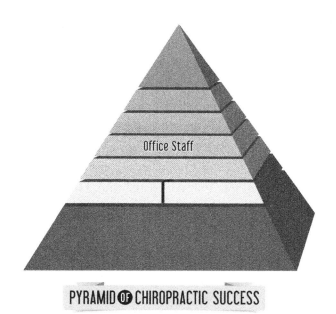

PYRAMID OF CHIROPRACTIC SUCCESS

"You can't grow your business without growing your people."

—Donald Cooper

Your front office receptionist is almost as important as the doctor in an office. Not in that they are the leaders and that patients will listen to what they say. But, your front office employees are the first contact that patients have on the road that leads to you. New patients will call your office, but they will reach the staff, not you. If they reach you, you have a bigger problem than this book is designed to fix. Doctors should never answer the phone, except if no one else is there, and maybe not even then.

Your staff must always have an attitude of, "How can I help you?" Potential patients interpret so much from the tone and attitude of your front office staff, even when staffers haven't said anything wrong. The tone of a crabby staff is worse than a staff member who says all the wrong things. If your staff does not always have a smile on their face and a song in their soul, they are not the right ones for the job.

Staff must never complain in front of patients. I had one staffer years ago who developed headaches and got into the habit of telling patients that she was hurting. What patient in their right mind would come to a chiropractor where the staff can't get rid of a headache? I am aware that chiropractic care can't treat all types of headaches, but patients don't know that.

Patients would be thinking, "Maybe this doctor is not very good." Even if they were not thinking negative thoughts about you, that patient came into your office to talk about them, not hear everything about your clerk's problems. You have to keep the emphasis on the patient, not on your problems.

Your staff must always wear proper attire. There are many different books written on the virtues of uniforms, and there are counter thoughts that more casual clothing sets a friendlier tone. I give my staff too much latitude, and I know it will be my downfall. In the past, I enforced polo shirts with our logo. It wasn't extremely formal, but it was uniform. In addition to the neat and professional appearance, my staff then became a walking billboard whenever they were on the town during lunch breaks.

You have to train your staff on what not to say. Patients have no idea what the limitations of your staff are, so they will ask then the strangest questions. Of course, they will ask insurance questions and questions about your schedule. But patients will also ask your staff about health questions and biochemical questions about vitamins and nutrition.

Your patients have no idea that you probably hired your staff right off the street. They have no experience or medical knowhow. It is easy to teach your front staff not to answer questions that are outside of their specialty but it is much harder to teach them effective communication skills.

You have to spend a lot of time training your front staff on how to properly communicate with patients. Just recently, I was in a chiropractor's office assisting him, and I asked his staff how they would handle a patient calling and wanting to cancel their scheduled visit. What I heard was horrible. It was no wonder the doctor was having problems getting his schedule filled. What they said went something like this:

"Mrs. Jones, would you like for me to reschedule that for you? "

If you ask a question in that manner, the answer will always be, NO. Have you ever gone into a furniture store looking to buy a new couch and as you went in, a sale associate stepped up and said, *"May I help you find something?"* What is your answer? NO. Why? You are looking for a couch, and you do need help, but you still said no.

It is the natural instinct to answer an open ended, yes-or-no question with no. I don't know why. Maybe it is the way we were all raised, or maybe it is in our genes. I have no idea, but we all say NO.

I gave them a few pointers on how to possibly do it better. The dialogue should go something like this:

Mrs. Jones: *I would like to cancel my appointment that I have for tomorrow, please.*

Staff: *Mrs. Jones I am sorry to hear that. Is there something wrong?*

Mrs. Jones: *No, something just came up, and I have to go out of town for a week.*

Staff: *Okay, no problem Mrs. Jones. I see that you normally come in the mornings. I am looking at the doctor's schedule for the week that you get back, and he has a 9 a.m. on Monday, January 15th or 10 a.m. on Tuesday the 16th. Which one would you prefer?*

Mrs. Jones: *Let's do the Monday at 9 a.m.*

That's how you handle a cancellation. That is a big difference compared to "Would you like for me to reschedule you?" You don't speak in open-ended questions. You look at Mrs. Jones scheduling trend and give her two options. And 99 times out of 100, she will pick one of those times, and show up.

You have to be a leader to your staff just as you have to be a leader to your patients. Staff would like a clear path on what their responsibilities are, and where they are going. I have a small procedural manual that workers have to read and sign, so they are aware what is expected from them.

Give your staff more work than they could possibly do, but prioritize the list for them. If you tell them which task is more important, they will follow your lead.

Before you give your staff heaps of work, make sure that they know how to do what you ask, and, if possible, why you are asking them to do it. There is nothing more frustrating than being given a job in which you have no idea where to start, what to do, why you're doing it, and then be chastised by a boss for not completing the work. Nobody will follow you blindly for too long without quitting. Your position is not to make their life more difficult, but to have a synergistic office atmosphere. People need direction and leadership.

Employees are like everyone else in that they want to feel appreciated for a job well done. If you have a staff that challenges you at every turn, you are either not being a strong enough leader or you have a person who is not fit to work for you. Some people are a better fit in another job, and I feel no shame in letting employees go to find themselves a better-suited career.

You have to bring your staff to seminars and train them constantly. If you do not train them, how can you look them in the eyes on Monday, after a weekend seminar, and tell them they are part of a team when you are obviously not treating them like a team. Taking staff to seminars will boost morale more than a pay raise ever could.

To foster the team atmosphere, you must also have staff meetings regularly. Ask their opinion about what could change in the office, so things can move more efficiently, effectively or faster. Before you make a change to procedure or protocols, make sure you get their feedback and possible pitfalls to the implementation that you may not have thought about.

Learn to reprimand problem behaviors quickly. But you must be doubly generous with your compliments. If they got a six-month-old bill paid that they have been working on, say, "Good job—now let me by lunch for everybody." I don't care if you are a child, a pet, patients, or staff. We all crave compliments and rewards. There is no substitute for a pat on the back or a rub behind the ear (if you are the family dog).

We don't lose our need for compliments simply because we grew up. We all need to celebrate our wins. That creates the stage for more winning. Basketball and baseball players all pat each other on the back, or butt, for anything positive. It could be a score, an assist, a rebound, or a good pass. They look for anything as a reason to give positive reinforcement, because they know that is what keeps the energy level high and makes people want to perform even better.

One of the best inventions in the world was profit sharing. I started this about six years ago, and I think it was one of the best things that I ever did. When I started the profit sharing, I cut out all raises. That has done two wonderful things. First of all, the staff is motivated to do better. The better the office does, the better they do, and that gives them quantifiable goals to reach.

Secondly, it eliminated tough financial months in my

office. No matter how big and successful your office will become, you will have months where the collections are great and months where you don't know how you are going to make the ends meet. Welcome to running a business. Now when collections are low, my payroll is low, which decreases my stress.

They also have a base wage, because I am not naive to the fact that they also have bills and I don't want them not to be guaranteed a base wage. Their profit sharing is graduated in that their percentage goes up as the collections go up.

Be sure that any system of profit sharing in your office is truly a reflection of profit. I have heard of doctors giving bonuses in the office based on other factors such as new patients, number of phone calls, or any other number of factors. That is dangerous ground, because there is a cost to doing business. And when you give money away to a staff for getting a new patient in the door, that patient may have the worst insurance in the world, or not pay their bill. Now you have paid out money to a person with no real gain to the business.

My profit sharing is set above a level that I know I need to run the office. If it takes $25,000 for you to run your office each month, then profit sharing should be placed on dollars collected above what is needed to run your office. That way, you are always assured not to be getting poorer as your staff gets richer.

I also constantly make up games for my staff. For instance, if they collect above $65,000 this month, I give them each a $150 gift card to whatever they choose. We have also set big six-month goals, and I have taken my staff, including their entire families, on trips to Mexico and cruises. All expenses paid. Those goals are set high, but I am happy to say they have earned it 3 times in the past few years.

All of these tactics, strategies and leadership skills help develop rapport with your employees. We have a clear chain of command, but we are also like family. We have fun, but we don't kid ourselves. We know it is a job and it has to be done correctly.

I believe that it was published by the small business association that the main reasons why employees don't like their job and eventually quit is:

1) I don't feel trusted or valued
2) I don't enjoy who I work with
3) I'm not proud of what I do

Knowing these reasons, it should be easy to create an atmosphere conducive to work and fun. Don't try to reinvent the wheel. Create an environment that allows your staff to feel valued and trusted, where they can enjoy who they work with and be proud to work for a chiropractor. Recognize where each staffer has gifts and are great, and give them jobs that are paired with their personality. Give them the opportunity to show off their greatness. But, remember there is no cure for incompetence. Learn to hire quickly and fire quickly.

Employees can be tough, especially if you have a soft heart. No one likes to fire a person. I have to say that it is my least favorite thing to do, but if a ship is sinking, the captain must throw over all cargo that is not absolutely necessary for survival. No one likes to do it, but it has to be done to save the ship.

There are hundreds of things done behind the scenes to

keep a chiropractic office running smoothly. There is no way that the doctor could treat patients, keep up on paper work and still do the hidden work. You need effective emplyees who can assist you. This reliance on staff, however, can create an interesting paradigm within the workings of your office. If you rely on people too much, you can feel trapped. Employees must never feel like you need them more than they need a paycheck.

How can a leader fire a person that they rely on so heavily? The answer is simple, and allows you to kill two birds with one stone. Create a procedure manual. One is that it decreases your reliance on any one staffer. And second, it allows you to create a system in your office that allows it to function in your absence, if you decide to go on vacation or sell the office in the future.

Every staff in a smoothly functioning clinic must submit a list of all activities they do. Everything from answering phone calls to collecting past due insurance payments. No matter how small and insignificant that activity might seem, they must bring that list to you, and you are to review the list together to ensure that nothing was left out. Once you have agreed on the list of activities, they are to construct a procedure on how each situation is to be dealt with in an effective and courteous manner. Once employees have fully described each of their tasks, it is ready for your review. If it meets your approval, you have just created a procedure manual for each of your employees.

Once a procedure manual has been created, you are no longer trapped by employees that have a poor attitude. There will be some difficulty in firing bad employees, but new recruits can be trained much more rapidly and more effectively. As stated earlier, this will also allow you to create a system of operations. This unique system is yours, so you can create a franchise model to open satellite offices or sell your office, when you are ready. Offices that are systemized suffer less loss in revenue when key personnel, like the doctor, leave the practice. This is very important to potential buyers when you are ready to sell.

Yes, employees can be a pain in the butt, and for that reason, many doctors hate to hire more staff. It is costly, you have to train them, and you may have to fire them someday. Instead, I want you to celebrate when you need a new staff person. If you need more people, it is because you are growing, and that is a great problem to have.

I believe this is also a great place to talk about associate doctors. Every time I go to a seminar, I hear other doctors talk about how the associate they hired was a lazy bum, and didn't want to work. And about how the new doctor could not follow orders, and had no general concept of what it took to grow an office.

I have also had my fair share of associates work for me over the years and hear the horror stories from the other perspective. I have heard about getting paid $10 per hour, about fighting with other associates in an office about who was to get the next new patient, and associates who were not allowed to talk to or treat patients. I have even heard the broken promises that the employer would sell the associate the clinic after five years, only for the associate to stay for six years with no end in sight. I have heard more lies and disrespect given to associate chiropractors than I have heard from any other profession.

I will attempt to write the remainder of this chapter to encompass both the employer and employee perspective.

A contract between a doctor and an associate must be a win/win relationship. The hiring doctor must feel that the new doctor is committed to the job, and has the work ethic needed to run a successful office. The new doctor must feel he or she is being properly compensated both with practical education and finances. If either party feels they are being taken advantage of, than that relationship will not last long.

However, if you want your office to continuously grow and not become a burden to you, as you get busy, you must hire an associate. Can the management of the new doctor be a pain? Of course! No one said that running a business was easy. But, if you want to grow your business, you need personnel to help you take that next leap.

If you are going to have a doctor who is straight out of school in your office, you must train them. The physician must be fully aware of what you expect from him or her, and you must teach them your protocols on how you expect patients to be treated, as well as show them proper billing, coding and scheduling. If you don't train them properly, you can't blame them when they screw up. You are the leader in your office, and it is about time you acted that way.

Make sure that this new doctor has a period through which he or she can earn a small wage while in training. This period should never be more than six months, because if they are not ready to see patients after six months of training, than you probably hired the wrong person. After the six-month learning period, the doctor should be switched to a percentage of collections.

I generally start with 35% of their collections, but I give higher incentives after certain milestones have been reached.

Any doctor who wants a base wage rather than a percentage should not be hired. A real go-getter will want the opportunity to expand, but the person who wants a base wage is only looking for a cushy job. This can be another indicator that you hired the wrong person.

In order to survive as an associate, you should be able to earn equivalent to what you have outstanding in your student loans. If you managed to rack up $150,000 in student loans, you will need to earn close to that amount each year. If you can't make that amount, you might want to look at working somewhere else.

Chiropractic associates are difficult for both the employee and the employer. There is generally a law-binding contract that not only features a no-compete clause, but also contains many other stipulations. Be sure that, as the employer, you get a lawyer to draft your contract. And as an employee, be sure that you get a lawyer to read over your potential contract. Contracts once signed may be difficult to terminate, and may cost you a lot of money and time to rectify.

Despite the negativities of being an associate chiropractor, or hiring an associate, it is a must if you wish to expand. New chiropractic students know virtually nothing about coding, billing, paperwork, or managing patients. And an internship in a successful chiropractor's office is the cheapest and best way to get the knowledge you need. From the employer's perspective, it is one of the only ways to expand a business and free some time to spend with family and possibly do some travel. It can be a nightmare, but if you do your due diligence and create a win/win situation, it can be one of the best things that happens for both parties.

6
Insurance

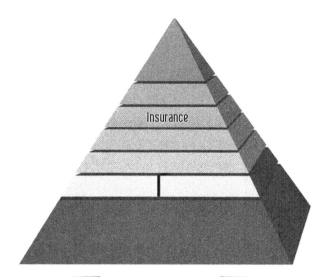

PYRAMID **OF** CHIROPRACTIC SUCCESS

*"To live and not be rich is a misfortune and it is doubly
a misfortune because you could have been rich just as
well as being poor. We ought to be rich if we can by
honorable methods … ."*

—Catherine Ponder

Insurance is the best and the worst thing that has happened to chiropractors. It is the worst in that chiropractors

are constantly micromanaged by third-party payers. We fill out gobs of paperwork, and the insurance carrier says we can see them for six visits, and we are allowed to do only one passive modality each visit. This is frustrating, to say the least, especially when we discover that these chiropractic management groups were created and run by other chiropractors. Most likely, these chiropractors could not make it in a patient practice and decided to be pencil pushers instead. It belittles what we are trying to do and makes the patient think that we are the ones doing something wrong when the procedures get denied.

However, insurance is also the best thing that has ever happened to chiropractors in that it initially gave us better acceptance. I say initially because back when insurance started accepting chiropractic services as a paid treatment, it opened the eyes of the world to the fact that chiropractic is no longer alternative, but necessary. However, now that card has been played out, and our acceptance in society can only grow from here, with or without insurance coverage.

Insurance also pays better than seeing patients for cash, provided, of course, that you know what you are doing. This higher fee for service and the ability to get paid for modalities above the chiropractic manipulation allows chiropractors to see fewer patients and still be able to run a lucrative business. This has allowed chiropractors to become philanthropic and become more recognized in charity work.

Lastly, insurance was good for the chiropractic profession in that it forced our profession to do something that we hate to do—and that is the art of doing great documentation. I have never met a chiropractor yet who liked to do notes, exams and reports. I have heard however, "I don't want to do all that stuff. All I want to do is adjust patients."

We all want to do our core competency and that is it. What a wonderful world that would be but that is not the world we live in. We live in a world that says, "If it is not written down, it didn't happen."

Insurance won't allow you to push on a patient and make a few chicken scratches on paper and charge for an exam. They have forced us to increase our standards. This is a good thing. We must first be better, and act better if we want to have better.

I am quite aware that insurance is going too far. Now we need time in and time out on every visit. We need not only to stretch a hamstring and write it down, but we have to time how long we did it to avoid audits. Insurance is pushing us too far, but we have to learn to push back with legislation and appeals. Life is most certainly not fair.

The main reason that the topic of insurance shows up on **The Pyramid of Chiropractic Success** is that it is something that can make your business income increase if you know what you are doing. It is much easier to get ahead if you are getting paid more for your services. Insurance varies dramatically from one area to the next and from one insurance carrier to the next. For example, Medicare pays almost double for a chiropractic adjustment in Alaska compared to most places in the continental United States. Because of this fact, practicing in Alaska and accepting insurance would create a much more lucrative practice compared to working in Idaho. I know the cost of living is more in Alaska, but that is beyond the scope of this book.

You by no means have to accept insurance in order to

be successful. I have been in many offices that accept no insurance, and they are booming. However, their lower fee for service is compensated for higher volume of patient treatment. As stated earlier, higher volume offices are fine, but it takes a really special person to see 200 patients in a day. As I mentioned, I once practiced that way when I lived in South America, and swore I would never do it again. I'm just not cut out for it.

I know insurance can be a pain in the ass. However, as a chiropractic coach, I would never take a doctor or a chiropractic office under my wing unless they accepted insurance. I say this for two main reasons:

1) Insurance can be a great source of income
2) I deal only with doctors who are in the chiropractic profession to help people, not only to do what is convenient or easy for them.

If you are in the profession to serve, you must ask yourself: Is the patient better served with accepting insurance or by not accepting it? Patients have paid for their insurance through premiums, and they want to get something for their effort. They want to use their insurance.

The doctor who recognizes this truth understands patients and the doctor's role in the service process. We have been called to this profession to serve, not to complain that insurance makes us fill out paperwork.

Every day, I receive an email about someone trying to push a cash practice. They tell me that they have the method to decrease all my stress. That may be true, but I am not in practice for me. I am in it for the patient. These seminars look appealing because we all know someone who got audited by an insurance office and lost. They have had to pay back possibly hundreds of thousands of dollars, and we think that if that had to happen to us, we would be out of business.

There is always a potential for audits when dealing with an insurance company. I don't want to sugar-coat the position you are in, but with all facets of life, there are risks. I know of many doctors who have been audited and lost big. And I know of cases in which physicians had to pay back only a thousand dollars.

When insurance comes knocking at your door, it is usually because you have been doing something very fishy. It costs the insurance company a lot of money to come to your office and audit your charts and billing procedure. If auditors are there, I can guarantee you they already know what they are looking for. They have analyzed your billing tactics, and have found many inconsistencies or errors that put them in your office in the first place.

If you are billing abnormally high, or if you are doing similar codes on every patient who walks in your door, you are putting yourself at risk of an audit. People are not the same, and their symptoms are not the same. So why is it that you think you can treat everyone the same? Or maybe you are doing too many timed codes inconsistent with your peer billing. These tactics show up very easily, and will get you into trouble. For instance, I knew a doctor who billed a level-five exam on all his new patients. He got audited and lost, resulting in him paying back almost $300,000. And then there was the guy who was getting a massage therapist to do a massage and bill the insurance four units of a manual therapy code. He got audited and had to pay back more than $100,000. These are all real stories. But trouble brewed only because on each occasion, the doctor was trying to do something illegal in order to make more money.

If you properly document everything that you do, justify why you did it, and don't do anything illegal or unethical, you will rarely have a problem with insurance companies. If you do it right, you will get more patients, and get paid well for seeing them.

To have less stress dealing with insurance companies, you must first change your attitude. The insurance companies are not out to get you. They are not always out to make your life harder. You have to think of it from their perspective. If you were the one paying the bill, wouldn't you want to know exactly what you were paying for and that the treatment was effective? They are not out to get you, but they will be the first one to call you about poor note taking and errors in billing. My philosophy is to do it right the first time. Then, you can sleep well at night, knowing you did nothing wrong.

I stated earlier that most chiropractors have an inherent hatred of taking notes, and I have to admit that I was once that way as well. I had to conquer this hatred, and this is how I did it. I now look at the treatment of the patient as my gift and service to humanity, and the note taking as my way that I get paid. I adjust patients for them and I write the note for me. The more I write, and the better I write, generally the more money I can collect for my services.

I realized that I don't only get paid for what I do, but for what I document. It is fraud to document procedures that were not performed, and I would never advocate such a practice. However, once I fully understood proper billing and coding, I realized that we generally do so much above the chiropractic adjustment, that we can get paid for in a patient visit. Discover how to bill and code correctly, and you can make a fortune.

Lastly, when dealing with insurance companies, you must fully understand the terminology and the legal ramifications. You must know what a deductible is, the difference between copay and a coinsurance, as well as maximum out-of-pocket expense. Patients must pay their copay, coinsurance, and deductible. To forgive a patient from these charges is considered baiting. Baiting means that you enticed the patients to enter into your office and not under their own volition.

Baiting may also be described as advertising for free or discounted services. Be very careful what you advertise as free. Your state board can better help you determine what is okay in your state.

Remember that the system we're discussing is not designed to make you fail. It is designed to help you succeed. You just have to know how to play the game.

7
Location

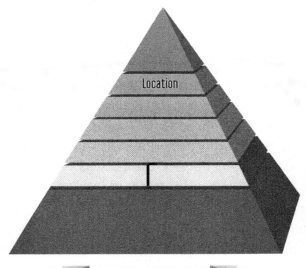

PYRAMID **OF** CHIROPRACTIC SUCCESS

"There are three things that matter in property: location, location, location."

—Lord Harold Samuel

The location of your office can make a difference to your success, at least in the initial start-up. I have an office in the parking lot of Wal-Mart, and since the day it opened, new patients have piled in. The only advertising that I had to do was put a banner in the window saying, "Accepting New Patients." I am delighted to find that location, because it has made my job so much easier. However, my most successful office is in the worst location, or so it appears. It is in a claustrophobic, downtown area with horrible curb appeal and poor signage.

This successful office was slow to get started, but once it got going, it took off like a rocket, and we have never looked back since. The difference is that the doctors in the downtown area are dedicated, hardworking, personal, and chiropractic leaders. That office has been open for 10 years, and they are seeing 1,000 patients per month, and have been for five years now. I could move that office to the worst area of town, and it wouldn't make a difference.

My point is that the physical location does make a difference—but only during the initial start-up. That is why it is on **The Pyramid of Chiropractic Success**. But that is also why it is near to the least important aspects. Great locations will give you a lot of traffic, and that is great. But once everyone in town knows where you are, the location will make little difference. As we stated in the beginning part of this text, the doctor and his or her attitude is what ultimately makes or breaks an office.

Another question I am often asked is: Where should new chiropractors set up? Should they choose a big city or should they shoot for the small town? That question can be difficult to answer, because it greatly depends on the doctor's attitude. If the physician is a person who enjoys a big city and will feel more at home in the city, then a city is where he or she should set up shop.

On the other hand, if they are small-town folk, than they

should go more rural. If the doctor has no preference, and is willing to go anywhere to be successful, I will give them my opinion. I believe that small towns are the better choice. My most successful offices have always been in towns with a population of about 20,000 to 50,000 people, but have a draw from more rural areas.

Offices in smaller towns can be difficult because there are only so many patients to go around, and usually, there are other chiropractors already there. My best office is in a town of about 20,000 people, with a draw of about 200,000 people from neighboring small towns and farmland.

Let me show you my logic. Chiropractors in larger cities rarely get noticed. There are hundreds of chiropractors competing for the same patients, and the only way they know how to compete is through advertising. Advertising in cities is much more expensive when compared to rural areas. Yellow Pages ads can be 10 times the price, and billboards can soar to 50 times the price of costs in rural areas. Generally, the city chiropractor who has the biggest budget wins.

If you are initially setting up an office, I doubt you have the money to have the luxury of a large budget. Next, it is harder to connect to key people in cities. Key people can make your business overnight, and it is highly unlikely you will be best buddies with the mayor of Chicago.

In smaller towns, you can personally know the mayor, the head of the chamber of commerce, key radio personalities, and important business people. All of these key individuals can put you on the map. They will spread your name over town quickly, if they like you. One key reminder: If they don't like you, they can destroy you. So, no matter what you do, make sure they like you. Do this right and before you know it, you will be one of those influential people in the town.

Rural towns also have cheaper rent, less expensive staff, better parking, and more personable patients. It can be hard enough to succeed in practice. So why make your struggle more difficult than it needs to be? Start up in a small town.

This section is also an appropriate area to talk about what the appearance of your office should look like. When it comes to your office appearance, patients can make judgmental, illogical decisions, and they make them quickly. The appearance of your office will tell a potential patient something about who you are. If it speaks well they will transfer that judgment to you. If your created atmosphere somehow speaks poorly, they will also judge you in that light.

There are many thoughts about how a professional office should look. Some say that you should set it up sterile like a hospital. This theory holds that the posters should be medically based, and chiropractic slogans should be plastered throughout. Others believe that your office should look more like an art gallery with bold colors and professionally framed art.

To answer the question more accurately, we must look at the office from the patient's perspective, because who really cares what *we* think? First, we have to consider what the potential patient is looking for. Are they really looking for a chiropractor, or are they actually looking for relief from their symptoms? They are, of course, looking for symptom relief. Does an image of false teeth in a glass on a poster that states "What will you do when your spine wears out?" really scream symptom relief? Not really, and it may cause younger, potential patients to feel left out.

When I first opened a practice out of school, I had all of these pro-chiropractic posters plastered all over my walls, but I noticed that they simply became wallpaper. Nobody ever asked me about what the iceberg poster really meant or what the false teeth in the glass was supposed to imply. I think that if your posters on the wall are not being talked about, then maybe you don't need them. If you don't need them, take them down.

I believe that it is more important that you have an office that exudes comfort, relaxation and health. That is what new patients are looking for. The chiropractic propaganda is mainly designed to transfer patients to wellness care, and the first day is not the time for that message.

I paid an interior designer to walk through my office and give me suggestions on what color of paints should be on which walls and what type of paintings I should proudly display. Most of my anatomical charts and chiropractic posters are long gone. I have gotten so many more compliments about how my office has looked since the transformation that I know I made the correct choice.

Besides, many patients, especially women, are knee-deep in today's HGTV-inspired design era, and they are learning that some areas, offices and rooms really are more psychologically inviting than others because of warmer colors and artistic balance. For proof, look no further than earthy-oriented, Starbucks-style coffee bars, which often attract people for frothy drinks, yes, but also for simple relaxation and unwinding.

Most patients are not looking for a chiropractor when they come into my office, even though I am one. What they are looking for is relief, pure and simple, and someone told them they would find that with me. So, in essence, what they are buying is me, or, in your case, you. You first must sell you and then you sell them wellness care and the philosophy of chiropractic. By dealing with patients in that manner, you have much less problem getting them to follow acute treatment and much fewer obstacles transitioning them to wellness care.

I understand that the above statements, much like most statements in this book, are simply my opinion. There are many opinions on how your office should look, and they can all be valid. Remember, this is the second-to-last important topic on **The Pyramid of Chiropractic Success**. It is nowhere near as important as many of the other topics previously discussed, and for that matter, you can succeed with either a traditional-looking office or with my art gallery appearance. That is, of course, if you master all the steps closer to the base of the pyramid.

8
Technique

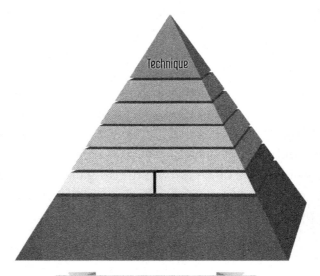

PYRAMID ⊙F CHIROPRACTIC SUCCESS

"All work is empty save when there is love; and when you work with love you bind yourself to yourself, and to one another, and to God."

—Kahlil Gibran

Lastly, we enter into the hot topic of chiropractic technique. Whenever I interview prospective associates, they always want to talk about what techniques I use, and then they usually want to impress me with their bag of tricks. Little do they know, with few exceptions, that I could care less about their technique. You can tell that they are asking themselves if they believe they are a good fit for my office. They may or may not be a good fit for my office, but technique is not the determining factor.

In school, we constantly dealt with the technique wars. You know what I mean! My technique is better than your technique. We sound like children arguing over a baseball game. I have heard upper-cervical doctors say, "I pity the person who has had their neck wrenched on with general manipulation." Thompson doctors bash Gonstead doctors for turning patients on their side and "cracking" a patient's back, while Gonstead doctors think everyone else is a bunch of pansies. Who's right? Who's wrong?

We made such a big deal of technique in school that when we graduated, we took our prejudices with us, believing that a patient cared. Patents care only about one thing: getting well. If you make your speech to the patient only about the glories of your technique, they will soon leave. The reason they leave is because your office is not supposed to be about you. It is supposed to be about the patient. Patients want you to take their needs into account, not your ego.

When a person attends an art school to study painting, acting, or pottery, the school will teach them several techniques to perform their art. Chiropractic is much the same. While in college chiropractors will learn the art of chiropractic adjusting as well as the science and philosophy of the chiropractic profession. But, similar to art school, chiropractors are not taught to sell their skills. They are taught only to perfect their skills. I do not blame the schools for this shortcoming. I do not see it as the school's responsibility to teach what patients and employers are looking for any more than art schools teach painters how to sell their art.

In general, chiropractors are artists, not business people, so they believe that the key to chiropractic success is to be highly skilled in their technique. And if they are failing in a practice, they believe they should learn more clinical skills and technique. Is this true? It has not been my experience.

Artists of all shapes, styles and skill levels have sold paintings that I believe to look like kindergarten creations. When it comes to art, everyone has his or her opinion on what is good. This is the same regarding the chiropractic artist. I have seen successful doctors who have, what I believe, horrible skills. And I have seen highly skilled doctors struggle. Why? Because technique has little to do with success!

With all of my experience dealing with other doctors, I can tell you when technique does matter. The first situation is when a patient comes into your office looking for the same thing that they are used to, and also when a patient leaves another doctor because they are too aggressive. For example, I have had the privilege of treating many blue-collar workers who have been to other doctors and gotten generally manipulated in their lumbar spine on both sides.

This is not a procedure I do in my office because I like to be specific in my adjustments. However, if I do not give them what they expect, it is very possible they will not return for further treatment. If the patient has had good results with that type of care, you may think about repeating what you know works. Or, if you are really skilled in your conversational methods, you can convince them to do it your way. But, that is risky business.

Another similar example is when a person decides to leave a chiropractor he or she has seen for years to see you because they have been adjusted very forcefully. "Every time I go there, he hurts me," the patient says, "and I have heard that you are much less forceful."

This person is searching for a lighter technique, so you would be wise to accommodate him or her and not adjust them with much force. The key in both of these cases is to give the patient what they want, not what you want. If you listen carefully, you can determine the most appropriate way to handle each case.

The second example of when I see that the type of technique matters is when a doctor steps outside of the normal box on what is generally expected as chiropractic. I have no need to degrade any technique, because I believe that there are many ways to heal the spine. But non-traditional techniques generally fail to maintain a higher volume of patients. Let's say that you decide to practice upper-cervical specific chiropractic only in the city of Chicago. Many patients have a difficult time coming to grips with you adjusting their neck when they have low back pain. However, due to the large population, you will convince enough patients and you may thrive. If, however you plan to practice upper cervical exclusively in a town of 15,000 people, you will never convince a large enough volume of people to have a thriving practice. It is simply too far out of the box for most patients. So stay within expected definitions of chiropractic if you decide to live in a rural area.

I love to keep many different tricks up my sleeve. I practice many techniques, and I am constantly adding more. When you have many ways to fix a patient, you have more options, and therefore are capable of fixing more people. I practice light techniques such as activator and Thompson, and I practice more forceful techniques such as diversified and Gonstead.

While talking to a new patient, I try and get the sense as to what technique they would most enjoy. If I sense that they would like lighter techniques, I will say, *"Mary, I can fix your problem two different ways. One is lighter but generally takes more visits, and another one that may be more painful for you but generally works faster. Which do you prefer?"*

If she states that she would like to go the lighter one, and on the sixth visit she states, *"Doc, why is this taking so long?"* then you now have a way out. You can remind her that you asked her in the beginning of treatment, and she took the longer road. Her slow recovery is not your fault.

Learn as many techniques as you can to assist you in treating patients. But never fall in love with a technique. You may believe that one is better, but that is egotistical and subjective. The most successful offices are the ones making the care about the patient and not about the doctor.

9

Long-Term Wealth

"You will become rich when you do rich people stuff with your money. If you do poor people stuff with your money, you will become poor people."

—Dave Ramsey

I have covered all aspects of the Pyramid of Chiropractic Success, but I thought it fitting to add one additional chapter to this book. It is the topic of long-term wealth.

It is not enough that I teach doctors how to have busy, successful offices that are tremendously lucrative. It is also important that I teach the necessity of growing financially as you mature. This topic is near and dear to my heart because I did not personally discover the importance of long-term wealth until later in my career, and it dramatically slowed my progress.

I was born in a very poor family, and when I became successful in practice, the money went straight to my head. I bought fine cars, yachts, farms, mansions, and went on many very high-priced vacations. I figured that all of my work was finally paying off, and I was going to spend every dollar I made. After 10 years of spending, the thrill started to dissipate, and I soon realized that I had no money saved.

My emotional state became beaten down because I felt like I worked for 10 years and had little to show for it. I tried to sell the yacht, and discovered that I could not sell it for enough to pay off the loan I still had remaining. I tried to sell my mansion, and soon found out that it is difficult to sell a $2 million home. I discovered the truth in the statement that "anything is worth only what someone is willing to pay for it."

I decided I needed a large savings account to make me feel like my last 10 years was worth it. I am by no means indigent, but I was trying to recoup some of the money I spent over the years through a quest to put money in savings. It did not work as I had hoped.

I swore that from that day forward, I would start saving money. The next 10 years would not be like the last. I needed a formula that would start me on the road to wealth and financial freedom. In the book, "The Richest Man in Babylon," George Clason illustrates the importance of saving. He believes that in order to be rich, one must save 10% of earnings to be in position to create wealth. He says that percentage can be invested to grow, but only in low-risk or guaranteed-growth funds.

I was behind in my savings. I needed to find low-risk, high-growth investments, and I needed to put away more than 10% to make up for lost time. I started doing research on the best ways to compound my savings, in the hope that I could gain back some of the lost savings. The remainder of this chapter is dedicated to what I discovered in the quest so that you might learn from my mistake. I want you to retire a very wealthy chiropractor.

I decided that the best way to tackle the problem was to work backward. I am currently living well, and I want to be living equally as well when I retire. So I had to first determine the amount I needed to retire while keeping my current lifestyle. I bought a book to aid me in this calculation, and what I discovered shocked me as I am sure it will shock you.

I will not divulge my current income. Instead, I will choose an arbitrary figure as my starting point, and you may do a similar calculation with your income. For this explanation, I will start with an individual making $150,000 a year. This is no great salary for a doctor, but at least a respectable amount.

The next part of the equation is to determine inflation. Inflation is the amount of devalue that your money has over time. We all know that it takes more money to live today compared to 50 years ago. So that's inflation. Inflation ranges from year to year, but averages three to four percent. It has been higher more recently, and will continue to rise as long as the government devalues our dollar by continuing to print more money.

However, if we stick with the long-term average of three to four percent, we can determine that it takes approximately 20 years for our money to be worth half of what it is worth today.

Finally, you need to estimate your lifespan to determine the amount of money you need to retire. This can be a scary undertaking, because no one likes to think about dying. But let's be real in stating that we can't live forever. With today's modern medicine and the fact that you are a chiropractor (which means, I hope, that you live and eat healthily) it can be assumed that you may live into your 90s.

Becoming old and broke is a common fear. So, for this explanation, I will assume that you will live to be 95 years old before you die. Let's say that it takes a while for you to become successful in your office. So, you start saving money at the age of 35. That equates to 60 years of either work or retirement that you will need to save money for. Another way to say this is that you will go through three cycles of inflation, each cycle being equal to 20 years.

The calculation for determining the amount of money that you will need at age 95 to live at your current level of lifestyle is calculated as follows. Take note that after each 20-year cycle, you will need two times the money to live at your current standard.

Current income X 2 = money needed at 55 years old
55 year old income X 2 = money needed at 75 years old
75 year old income X 2 = money needed at 95 years old

Now, let's place the real numbers from our scenario with the above calculation to determine the amount of money you will need at age 95.

$150,000 X 2 = $300,000
$300,000 X 2 = $600,000
$600,000 X 2 = $1,200,000

The point of this calculation is that if you are currently 35 years old and earning $150,000 a year, and believe you will die at age 95, you will require $1,200,000 each year to live the same way you are currently living.

This calculation was an extreme eye opener for me, as I hope it was for you. This calculation does not account for variables such as federal and state taxes, which further complicates the calculation and makes it even worse.

Whenever financial advisors talk about taxes and retirement, it is common for them to state that you will be in a lower tax bracket when you retire. But when you think about it that cannot be logically true. You will have fewer tax deductions because you will probably have no dependents and you will more than likely have your house paid off. Next, you will be earning $1.2 million a year, not $150,000, which will put you in a higher tax bracket. Lastly, whenever I ask people whether they believe taxes will be higher or lower in years to come, they always say higher.

When financial advisors figure the amount you will need to maintain your current lifestyle, they also tell you how much you can remove from your IRA, or 401K without dwindling your principle. This is just a fancy way of saying that they want you to live off of the interest that you gain each year so you can live on your savings into perpetuity.

Feel free to do their calculations to prove my point. But believe me that you cannot possibly save enough money in your working years to retire at even 70 years old and still be collecting $1.2 million per year when you are 95 years old. 401Ks and IRAs will never get you to where you need to be.

However, let's not be stupid here. Assuming you are working for someone else, and they are going to offer a 401K that your employer will match, any employee would be stupid to turn down free money. Take your employer's money and match but only the minimum. You have to find a more lucrative way to save the amount of money you need via other methods, but never turn down free money.

The biggest pitfall one soon discovers is the problem of taxes. If you could only find a way to not pay taxes on the money once you withdraw it after retirement, it would dramatically reduce the amount you would need to live comfortably. Let's perform the previous calculation again. But, this time, let's do it with after-tax dollars. If you are currently making $150,000 a year, you are in an approximately 40% tax bracket if you count all state and federal taxes. That means you really live on only $90,000 a year. If we did not have to pay taxes after retirement, we could use this $90,000 figure to extrapolate our needed income at age 95.

$90,000 X 2 = $180,000 at age 55
$180,000 X 2 = $360,000 at age 75
$360,000 X 2 = $720,000 at age 95

Collecting $720,000 a year seems a whole lot easier compared to $1.2 million. The next wisdom I had to search for was how could I save money and still pay no taxes after retirement. There are only two ways to accomplish this goal and that is Roth IRAs and maximally funded, or maximum-funded life insurance contracts. In both instances, one must use post-tax dollars to fund these entities. But as one of my friends once said, "If you were a farmer, would you rather be taxed on seed price or the price of the harvest?" The answer is obvious—that we would rather be taxed on the low cost of the seed compared to the compounding yield of the harvest.

Roth IRAs are very easy to set up. But I soon discovered that they were truly meant for lower-income citizens. The maximum I could place in this entity was $4,000 a year, which would never be enough to get the returns I was aiming for at age 95. Secondly, the government stated that once I made over a certain amount of money, I couldn't contribute to a Roth IRA at all.

It was disheartening to determine these facts, and I started to feel as if the government wanted me to save no money at all. Money saved means that it is not in circulation and therefore cannot be taxed. The government earns money via taxes, so I'm not surprised it was going to make my saving enough a difficult task.

I was very nervous about getting involved with a life insurance company as a means to save money. I already owned term life insurance, and I was locked in at a great rate due to my youth and excellent health. I always thought that to purchase life insurance as a savings account was for less intelligent people. The returns I was always quoted in the past were nowhere near what I was quoted from financial advisors selling mutual funds.

That was before I realized that life insurance was tax-free, while mutual funds would be taxed once I withdrew the money. As you saw from the above calculations, paying taxes dramatically changes the amount needed to live in later years.

I discovered that maximally funded life insurance was the only tax-free retirement savings still remaining for wealthy Americans. All other retirement accounts either grew only to be taxed when you withdrew the funds, or never allowed me to contribute enough funds to create a sizable nest egg.

A portion of the funds that I deposited into the maximally funded life insurance went toward the purchase of life insurance, while the remainder will be used to grow for retirement. I did not want the life insurance option, but legally, it had to be a part of the contract.

When I worked with a professional insurance agent who was highly skilled in the creation of these accounts, he calculated the minimum that had to be allocated to life insurance, as set by law. This allowed for the majority of money I deposited yearly into my contract to go toward growth rather than life insurance.

With permission from my insurance agent who is skilled in setting up these types of retirement accounts, I am at liberty to print his company name and address. For more information in creating your own account, please contact Doug Andrews and the Missed Fortune team at www.missedfortune.com.

Mr. Andrews taught me everything I needed to know about saving money for retirement and leaving large sums to my family once I pass away. He gave me hope for my financial future, and allowed me to contribute enough funds to make up for the lost time during the period when I did not contribute any funds toward my long-term financial wealth.

There are, of course, other ways to solidify your net worth besides retirement funds. Businesses that you create are worth money, and are always calculated by banks as net worth. Likewise, any equity you have in your house also increases your financial value. However, one must never over estimate the value of these assets. The true value of any asset is what someone is willing to pay for such assets.

Your chiropractic office may be collecting a million dollars a year, but let's not kid ourselves. No one in his or her right mind would pay a million dollars for an asset that hinges on your personality. The reason your office is successful is because of you, and if you sell it, the value will instantly diminish.

There are ways to increase the value of an office that I teach my clients. But it goes beyond the scope of this book.

With respect to the value of your home, and any equity you may have in it, we know that the housing market is constantly being reevaluated. Therefore, your home may be worth $400,000 one year, and five years later, be worth only $250,000. Equity in your home is only a paper value until the day you refinance it or sell it, at which time it has true value. Your home is not a good place to hold your money, because it is not as secure as you think.

The point that this chapter is trying to make is that if you work hard all of your life, you should have something to show for it. When you are old you should have more than just material possessions. You need long-term wealth. You will also notice that when your financial net worth increases as you age, your stress levels will decrease. Money becomes less of a concern when you have a large bank account. When you have a large bank account, you can still go to work and practice the way you want to rather than doing it a certain way because you have to.

Trust me. It feels great.

10
Closing Remarks

"Unfortunately there is no tomorrow. It is only found in the calendars of fools."

—Og Mandino

Chiropractic is a wonderful profession and, much like the priesthood, many are called to it. In the past, many chiropractors made great sacrifices that allowed us to have the freedoms we enjoy today. Some even went to jail for what they believed in. Our American and chiropractic system is set up for success.

Insurance pays well. Workers compensation and auto insurances pay for chiropractic care, and our acceptance by the general population has never been higher. We no longer have to struggle. All we need are some basic skills. Skills we were not taught in school.

Other successful businesses require these skills and other health care professionals demand them. If we don't learn, we will go to the way of the Dodo. Take your calling and your life seriously, and together, we can all succeed.

Remember the stunning stat from early in the book: Only three out of every 10 chiropractors who graduate are still in practice three years later. Those who survive longer than three years are not thriving, but are barely making ends meet. Only a few in thousands are really successful. As a profession, we have not done a good job at showing our true capacity.

Once the business of health care sees the lucrative aspect of chiropractic, we will be asked to be on staff at hospitals. Then and only then will we be able to share our passion for spinal adjustment worldwide and in a large meaningfully way.

If an individual chiropractor is not successful, one must assume that he or she is either lacking knowledge, skills, work ethic, motivation or the proper support structure. Some of these are personality flaws, and I have no desire to try and change a doctor's personality.

However, through the years, I have discovered that the doctor generally has the drive to succeed, the skills to succeed and the motivation. What they are lacking is the knowledge. They lack billing and coding knowledge, communications skills, success principles, they lack documentation knowledge, and most of all, they lack the business knowledge necessary to achieve success.

I remember back when I first graduated from chiropractic school, and I opened my first office. For the first two years, I struggled to get and keep patients, and to be honest with you, I was failing. I had many scapegoats. The economy was bad, the government didn't support small businesses, my school didn't educate me enough, my national and state associations were unsupportive, and I grew up in a family of modest means. In my mind, I had every reason not to succeed.

At one point, I returned to my chiropractic school for continuing education, and I saw more seasoned doctors driving BMWs and Mercedes Benz cars. They were wearing tailored suits and Rolex watches. I could not help but wonder what they knew that I didn't. They shared my government, state associations and educational background.

But yet they were obviously succeeding while I was struggling.

A few days later, I was standing in front of my mirror, at home getting a shave, when it occurred to me that I was an idiot. The reason I was not successful was not for any other reason except my own, personal lack. I was a straight-A student in chiropractic college. I always knew and stated that I would be successful, but now I had to admit the cold, hard truth that my failure was due to my actions and attitudes, not from the external environment.

Within two weeks, I noticed my office volume picking up. I went from seeing 50 patients a week to 80, and then, within a month, I was seeing more than 100 visits a week. I started looking for problems in my attitude, my communications with patients and my behavior. I started focusing more on building my mind rather than blaming my circumstance.

I now own and operate a million-dollar clinic and several satellite offices. Many doctors are working for me, and by most people's standards, I am rich. The funny thing about this story is that I got to where I am for several reasons. I live in a country that has a great government; I have a great state and federal chiropractic association to support me; my chiropractic education was second to none; and my humble upbringing has allow me to better communicate with my patients.

All of the things that I once blamed for my failure are now my biggest assets. All I needed was a mind shift. But I do know what it is like to struggle in the chiropractic practice, and that has helped me better relate to struggling doctors.

Chiropractic business success is a mental game, and therefore, any doctor wishing to succeed needs to have the proper blend of physical skills and metaphysical understanding. As seen in figure 8, on one side of the seesaw, you have metaphysical constructs showing the importance of mentally projecting what it is that you want out of life.

You have to have a great sense of self-worth, create goals and visualize the actualization of your goal. These concepts have been talked about by self-help gurus for thousands of years, but have only recently found their way into the business world. Yet, on the other side of the diagram, you have to be realistic by following concrete business practices that keep you grounded in reality.

If your patients perceive you as the person who is out on the fringe of the flaky or deeply metaphysical, they will have difficulty respecting you or following your recommendations. Yet, if you are purely physical, and believe only in things that are tangible, you will be missing out on a wealth of opportunity for business growth.

"Chiropractic is not mechanical. It is esoteric and mechanical."

—Larry Markson

Figure 8.

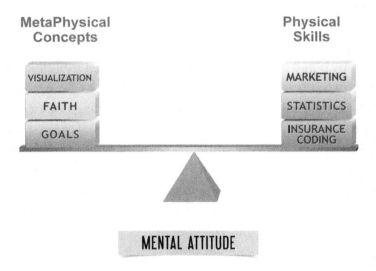

Successful living starts first with the proper mental attitude. It is first and foremost a way of thinking. It is not a physical or tangible thing. Thinking is meta-physical and does not become physical until your thoughts are put into action.

Have you ever noticed that your office grows after you come back from a seminar or after someone motivates you? I have noticed it many times, and likewise, my colleagues have often admitted it to me. Generally, after I speak to a chiropractor and I get them motivated, they also see this increase in patient volume as well as monetary collections.

Doctors are easily pumped and will expand rapidly. But because they have not truly figured out their true motivation, or as I said earlier, their WHY, they quickly become overwhelmed with the trials of everyday practice and then fall back into old ruts and old mental slavery. When they expand large enough and grasp the big picture of why they are a chiropractor and what their true motivation is, these ebbs and flows in practice become far less bumpy.

I expect that many doctors will see a boost in their business after reading this book. It will give them a clearer path and the desire to persist. But it will not last. In a couple of weeks, their patient volume and collections will drop back to their normal amounts. But let's get down to you: If you experience a boom followed by normal levels of business, you need a coach—someone capable of assisting you in continuous growth, to put you and keep you on the right track.

You need help to filter out your negative self-talk, your negative environment and create a system in your office that will lead you to success. You have to constantly put energy into your life or you will drift down to the lowest common denominator. You have to constantly be working at life or it will regress.

Young doctors are easily overwhelmed. The task of paperwork, insurance coding, and treating patients can frazzle the inexperienced. You have to learn to expand your mental capacity. God will never give you more than you can handle.

One day while assisting one of my clients who was new in practice, I pulled some of her charts and, looking at the name on the chart, I asked what John Doe's diagnosis was. To that question she replied, "I don't know. I'll need to look at the chart."

How is it that a new doctor who has only 50 patients and has been in practice two months could not possibly know what John's problem was off the top of her head? If you cannot file that many people in your head at any one time, how is it that you expect to be able to see 50 to 60 patients a day?

You have to be able to stretch your mind. You have to know what your patient's problems are off the top of your head. As you grow in consciousness, you will attract more people. If you think small, you will receive only a small life. But if you think big, you will experience all that life has to offer.

In the sequence of Be, Do, Have, you must first *be* something. You have to be a person of strong will and desire. You must be the person who sets goals and have a plan to actualize your dreams. You must be a person of high integrity.

You must be all of these first before you can do the job of chiropractic and run a successful business. Then and only then will you be capable of having the practice of your dreams, and all of the money and material items that come with it. Society will not allow you, or at least not for very long, to have the things you want without first requiring that you do something to earn your rewards. Let's not try and fool the laws of the universe, but instead, work within the known constructs of the system and use it to our advantage.

Owning and operating a chiropractic office is perhaps one of the hardest tasks I have ever done. To do it successfully, you have to wear many hats and fill big shoes. One minute, you have to be treating patients, and the next minute, you have to be worried about balancing bank accounts to prevent payroll from bouncing, or fixing a broken adjusting table. I will be the first to admit that it is not easy, and not everyone can balance so many tasks.

In the book, "The E Myth," Michael Gerber describes

the business world as having entrepreneurs, managers and workers. The clear lines of demarcation between each of these echelons allows for the average business to thrive. Entrepreneurs fulfill specific roles, managers have their part and the workers have a clear understanding of their responsibilities.

In the average chiropractic office, the doctor tries to fit in each level of the business structure, and that is difficult, and often leads to failure. However, it can be done, if you have the right leader. There is no shame in admitting to yourself that you can't balance all aspects needed to run an office. The key is to discover who you are. If you are not an entrepreneur, manager and employee all wrapped into one, it is okay. But if all you want to do is adjust patients, then, really, you should be an associate in an office you don't own.

The chiropractor-leader must learn to balance the management of the business side of the office with the technician aspect of practice. He or she must learn to delegate tasks that can be done by others. The doctor must take his role of leader very seriously and learn how to manage and motivate staff.

It is because of this weight that must be placed on the back of the doctor that I have observed, through experience, that it is the doctor's personality and attitude that are the main factors in operating a successful office. It is also why 75% of **The Pyramid of Chiropractic Success** is designated to the doctor.

Jim Rohn once said, "Failure is a few errors in judgment repeated daily." If this is true, and I believe it is, then success is simply a few things done right and repeated over time. The problem is that doctors generally don't know what those few things are. They think that if they have a good work ethic and keep doing what they are doing, then everything will work out fine.

If that were the case, we would have more successful chiropractors. Look—doctors have proven that they are hard workers by finishing eight years of school. I'm sorry to say a good work ethic is not enough. You need the right information and you need it now. Ignorance is not bliss. Ignorance is pain and failure. You have to recognize when your office is barely staying afloat, and what to do about it.

I have tried to understand why a struggling chiropractor would not seek outside help to grow their office, and I have tried to step into the shoes of the frustrated and broke chiropractor. Actually, that is not difficult, because I was once there myself.

I can remember feeling embarrassed, and inadequate. I remember feeling that it would be easier to quit and work for someone else than admit defeat to some chiropractic guru who was only going to judge me. I can assure you this is not the case. I would like to see you succeed so badly that I get emotional just thinking about it.

If you remember nothing else from this book, *please ask for help*.

I also understand that consulting firms that are designed to assist struggling chiropractors can be expensive. High cost is the last thing a struggling chiropractor needs. It is like kicking a man when he is already down. To remove that deterrent, I have created a program that is free to any struggling doctor.

I will analyze any office free of charge, and if I accept you as a client, I will get paid only if there is a boost in income. I do not want a piece of your company, and I will not take any money I do not help you earn. You have nothing to lose and much to gain.

It is human nature to want to expand. No one wakes in the morning and wishes they had fewer friends, less money or less influence compared to yesterday. The drive to expand is innate in the human species and very powerful. We want to give our children the things that we didn't have. We want to take our families on expensive vacations and drive beautiful cars. This is one of the reasons I say that all small business are family businesses. You can't leave work at the office and leave home at the home. If you are not successful, your family will know it. They know when you are stressed over money. If you have made promises to your family that you can't keep, it will cause tension both at home and at the office.

This drive to expand is what has advanced our society since the day we walked out of caves, and it will not change anytime soon. I know you want to grow. I know you want better things for your family. But, you can't keep doing what you are doing if you want a better life.

Charlie "Tremendous" Jones once said, "Life can be funny sometimes, but life is not a joke." You have to take your life seriously. Your problem is time, or, better stated, the lack of time. You have no time to mess around. Time is the only real asset we really have and every day that we are not progressing in business is lost time. And that is time that you can never recover.

Life gives us only a certain amount of time, and we have none to waste. You must become what you are destined to become, and you must live it now before your time runs out.

Have you ever tried to figure out how much you make per hour? If you made more money per hour, would you work more or would you take time to do the things you have always dreamed of doing? If you get into the rut of selling your time for money, you will eventually lose. Your family will eventually grow up and barely recognize you, and before you know it, you will be too old to enjoy life.

You cannot continue to sell your time. You must learn to leverage your time, your money, and your knowledge by leveraging staff and associates. Only then will you be able to have the life that you have dreamed about.

The average working person has between 30 and 40 years to save money for retirement, unless one expects to live on Social Security which is about $100 a month greater than being homeless. No wise person should expect or wish for the government to take care of them in their elder years. With that in mind, your peak earning years are dwindling, and you must act fast if you have any hope of saving enough to support your lifestyle.

Time waits for no one.

We must show the world that chiropractic is a great gift, and that we are highly skilled at selling it. However, we do not currently stand on that Promised land. The keys to success can be learned, and I would love to be the one to teach you. But, even if it is not my company you select, please find someone to help you.

If you are struggling, you are doing it needlessly. There are patterns of action that are consistent with success just as there are patterns of action consistent with failure. I can teach anyone the pattern to success, but I cannot instill desire or work ethic. The lack of these attributes is character flaws that are beyond my capacity to heal.

By now, I'm sure that you have sensed my attitude about the chiropractic business. I am about being real, authentic, taking responsibility and acting with integrity. I have no time for personal whining or blaming without taking action. I place no blame on things that I cannot control, because that mindset enslaves me. My life is for me to control and that liberates me. If you share my enthusiasm for chiropractic, and know that you can use this material for a breakthrough, please feel free to contact me.

You are not alone in your struggles. Too many chiropractors are failing in practice and are doing little to fight for their family business. Don't be that person. Look for help, whether from my company or any other. I don't really care which assistance you choose. When chiropractors succeed, we all progress as a profession. I am glad to be a part of the solution rather than a part of the problem, and I would love to take you along.

Let's make chiropractic practice success the norm rather than something abnormal.

Before I close, let me leave you a quote from my friend Keith Cunningham. He once told me, "Success should be non-negotiable. Which doesn't mean that you do the best you can. It means that you do whatever it takes."

I also leave you with a wish. I wish you all the success in the world, and that all your desires come true, and surpass your wildest dreams.

"Five years from now, you will be the same person you are today except for the people you meet and the books you read."

—Charlie "Tremendous" Jones

About the Author

Dr. Dennis Short was born in eastern Canada in a small fishing village. His widowed mother raised him, and two siblings, in a very modest house with little income. To the average outsider, he appeared to have no hope of living a successful life. He had little affluence and no male role model for guidance.

His grades in school showed promise, but his poor attitude, lack of drive, and desire to be the class clown generally landed him as a lower-B student.

An act of desperation and a lack of direction guided him to pursue a career at sea. He attended a college in the hopes of becoming a captain and sail the seven seas. The thought of visiting distant lands and living carefree sounded appealing at his young age. Yet, after a few months at sea, he quickly changed his tune. The constant rolling of the ocean and the hours of alone time was too much to bear.

His grades in the secondary academic world were much greater compared to high school. So he decided to return to college, but this time, to study marine biology. He took to the more difficult courses like chemistry, biology and mathematics like a duck to water.

At the Memorial University of Newfoundland, he found the key to his happiness was being the social butterfly. He loved the large classes and hundreds of fellow students. He made friends easily, and knew he could never be in a career where he spent hours alone like he did when he was studying on the sea.

Prior to graduation, he landed a well-respected job in marine biology with the Canadian government. He maintained this position for three years, until he realized the hundreds of hours alone looking through a microscope was not only ruining his eyesight, but also was not fulfilling his social personality.

He began to worry that no job would satisfy his personality and desires. After a period of anxiety and depression, he decided to look into the field of medicine. At this point, he had published research and his grades at the university were excellent, so it seemed like the next logical step.

He began to volunteer at the local hospital, and after two years of living the beginnings of a medical life, he had an epiphany. He states, "Why would anyone want to be a doctor? They work too many long hours, they are sleeping in the hospital rather than going home, and most are on their second divorce. God bless those who do it, but this life sucks."

It was at this low point in his life that a friend talked to him about chiropractic.

He knew nothing about it, but in a fit of despondency and lack of direction, he applied to Palmer College of Chiropractic, got accepted and was at the campus six months later. The very first time he was adjusted was in chiropractic school. He now admits that his decision to be a chiropractor was uninformed and crazy. But nevertheless, there he was.

"Chiropractic school was definitely the best time of my life. I loved the course work, I had hundreds of friends, and the philosophy of chiropractic rang true to my soul." However, like most chiropractic students, the separation from school and the realization of private practice resulted in a period of mental uneasiness.

During this time, the mental struggle was so great that it was difficult to focus on work, let alone grow a new business. The task seemed next to impossible. However, once he started to settle into his new life, he discovered that if he was to live the life of his dreams, he would have to take full responsibility for his success, or lack thereof. That is when his life and business started to soar toward greatness.

He has expanded his practice to include six offices, and many associate chiropractors. He has a beautiful, supportive wife and one son. He is enjoying the good life, living in a mansion on 100 acres, driving expensive cars, and enjoying his yacht on the lake. He is an icon for living the good life.

He claims, "Anyone can live well in America, as long as you do the correct thing in your business."

When asked why he became a chiropractor, he recognizes Gods plan. "I had no idea what chiropractic was. I left my country to go to a school with no idea what I was getting myself into. I can make no sense of it, so I must admit that God has brought me to this point. I can see no other rationale."

Dr. Short stresses that he is no one special. He points to his modest beginnings, stating, "If I can become successful, then anyone can."

He has most recently started a new chiropractic coaching company called **The Ultimate Chiropractor L.L.C.** The purpose of this company is to teach struggling chiropractors the art of operating a successful business. He recognizes that school trains doctors to be great chiropractors, but students are generally lacking in financial education. And that limits their potential for expansion. He wishes to bridge that knowledge gap for as many doctors as possible.

"When more chiropractors are financially successful, hospitals, which are operated by business people, will see the lucrative nature of chiropractic," he says. "Then, and only then, will we be asked to practice in hospitals. At that point, we will be able to treat more people and show the world the glory of chiropractic."

For more information on Dr. Short's vision, visit
theultimatechiropractor.com

Acknowledgements

Upon conception, God blessed each and every one of us with unique gifts. I have gotten to where I am by discovering and utilizing these gifts. I believe that I would have been successful no matter what profession or endeavor I decided to pursue. However, the chiropractic profession rings so true to my heart that I am delighted to have discovered the chiropractic principles. Without the intelligence and sacrifices of our founders no chiropractor would be practicing today. For that reason, I would like to take the time to salute every chiropractor that has aided in the development of our profession, which includes those that have been jailed for our beliefs. Their dedication will never be forgotten.

I would like to thank my mother who raised me to be a strong and determined individual. My father died when I was only a year old but she succeeded in keeping our family together. She was the one that taught me life would not be easy and that the hardest choices I have to make are usually the correct ones.

Thanks to my editor, Brian Blair, for correcting my awful grammar and syntax. Without you my message would never be comprehendible.

To my friends I would like to extend special thanks. You have helped me stay focused and on tract. One can succeed by oneself but the journey is sweeter when you have the love and support of friends. I see no need to list all of my friends you know who you are.

To all of my staff and specifically my office manager, Kim Mongeau, you keep my life on schedule and understand when it seems to take a different turn. You are the ones that I have come to count on.

Lastly, I would like to thank my wife, Callie. There are not a lot of women that would tolerate my ambition. You have been committed to me through the good times and the bad, which is the sign of true love. Life is more complete with you by my side. I hope that our love continues to grow as we age together.

One is capable of succeeding by oneself but the road is bumpier and much less enjoyable. With a strong, supportive team anyone can go further than they could by themselves.

Suggested Readings

The Big Leap, Gay Hendricks, Copyright 2009 by HarperCollins Publishers

Talking To Yourself Is Not Crazy, Dr. Larry Markson, Copyright 2008 by SPS Publications

The E-Myth Revisited, Michael E. Gerber, Copyright 1995 by HarperCollins Publishers

The Richest Man In Babylon, George S. Clason, Copyright 1926 by Signet

Missed Fortune 101, Douglas R. Andrew, Copyright 2005 by Warner business books

The Dynamic Laws Of Prosperity, Catherine Ponder, Copyright 2011 by Wilder Publications

Secrets Of The Millionaire Mind, T. Harv Eker, Copyright 2005 by HarperCollins Publishers Inc.

Think And Grow Rich, Napoleon Hill, Copyright 1960 by Highroads Media Inc.

Acres Of Diamonds, Russell H. Conwell, Copyright 1960 by Penguin Group

Rich Dad Poor Dad, Robert T. Kiyosaki and Sharron Lechter, Copyright 1997, Warner Books

Life Is Tremendous, Charlie Jones, Copyright 1968 by Tyndale House Publishes, Inc.

The Power of Your Subconscious Mind, Joseph Murphy, Copyright 2011 by Martino Publishing

The Success System That Never Fails, William Clement Stone, Copyright 2010 Wilder Publications, LLC.

The 7 Habits of Highly Effective People, Stephen R. Covey, Copyright 1984 by Free Press

The Road Less Travelled, M. Scott Peck, Copyright 1978 by Touchstone